Cambridge Elements

Elements in Politics and Society in Southeast Asia
edited by
Edward Aspinall
Australian National University
Meredith L. Weiss
University at Albany, SUNY

SOCIAL MEDIA AND POLITICS IN SOUTHEAST ASIA

Merlyna Lim
Carleton University

CAMBRIDGE
UNIVERSITY PRESS

Shaftesbury Road, Cambridge CB2 8EA, United Kingdom

One Liberty Plaza, 20th Floor, New York, NY 10006, USA

477 Williamstown Road, Port Melbourne, VIC 3207, Australia

314–321, 3rd Floor, Plot 3, Splendor Forum, Jasola District Centre,
New Delhi – 110025, India

103 Penang Road, #05–06/07, Visioncrest Commercial, Singapore 238467

Cambridge University Press is part of Cambridge University Press & Assessment,
a department of the University of Cambridge.

We share the University's mission to contribute to society through the pursuit of
education, learning and research at the highest international levels of excellence.

www.cambridge.org
Information on this title: www.cambridge.org/9781009548076

DOI: 10.1017/9781108750745

© Merlyna Lim 2024

When citing this work, please include a reference to the DOI 10.1017/9781108750745

First published 2024

A catalogue record for this publication is available from the British Library

ISBN 978-1-009-54807-6 Hardback
ISBN 978-1-108-71934-6 Paperback
ISSN 2515-2998 (online)
ISSN 2515-298X (print)

Social Media and Politics in Southeast Asia

Elements in Politics and Society in Southeast Asia

DOI: 10.1017/9781108750745
First published online: December 2024

Merlyna Lim
Carleton University

Author for correspondence: Merlyna Lim, Merlyna.Lim@carleton.ca

Abstract: This Element endeavors to enrich and broaden Southeast Asian research by exploring the intricate interplay between social media and politics. Employing an interdisciplinary approach and grounded in extensive longitudinal research, the study uncovers nuanced political implications, highlighting the platform's dual role in both fostering grassroots activism and enabling autocratic practices of algorithmic politics, notably in electoral politics. It underscores social media's alignment with communicative capitalism, where algorithmic marketing culture overshadows public discourse, and perpetuates affective binary mobilization that benefits both progressive and regressive grassroots activism. It can facilitate oppositional forces but is susceptible to authoritarian capture. The rise of algorithmic politics also exacerbates polarization through algorithmic enclaves and escalates disinformation, furthering autocraticizing trends. Beyond Southeast Asia, the Element provides analytical and conceptual frameworks to comprehend the mutual algorithmic/political dynamics amidst the contestation between progressive forces and the autocratic shaping of technological platforms.

This Element also has a video abstract: www.cambridge.org/ESEA_Lim

Keywords: social media, politics, activism, election, algorithms

ISBNs: 9781009548076 (HB), 9781108719346 (PB), 9781108750745 (OC)
ISSNs: 2515-2998 (online), 2515-298X (print)

Contents

1 Introduction

In Southeast Asia, separating contemporary politics from social media usage is unimaginable. The surfacing of mass rallies, whether located in the Independent Square of Kuala Lumpur, the National Monument of Jakarta, the Freedom Park in Phnom Penh, or other symbolic public spaces across the region, largely incorporates Facebook, Twitter (X), TikTok, and other social media platforms. Civil society organizations strategically curate attention-grabbing hashtags to gain public support, while hate groups exploit these platforms with hate speech and disinformation. Country leaders, including Prime Ministers Hun Manet of Cambodia and Lee Hsien Loong of Singapore, maintain social media accounts. Politicians and parties heavily depend on these platforms as primary campaign tools. While conventional campaigning methods like television advertisements, rallies, and banners persist, their efficacy is augmented by the proliferation of supporters' posts, comments, photos, and videos disseminated through social media channels.

The multifaceted utilization of social media has become indispensable to political communication, engagement, and information dissemination in Southeast Asia, shaping the dynamics of public discourse and political participation. As the region undergoes profound sociopolitical transformations, the pervasive influence of digital platforms emerges as a dynamic and manifold phenomenon, profoundly affecting the political fabric of diverse nations within this vibrant corner of the world. The intersection of social media and politics in Southeast Asia is paramount, necessitating an in-depth exploration of how digital technologies intricately shape political landscapes and vice versa.

Since its inception in 1994, the term "social media" has undergone various definitions. Over the years, the consistent theme in defining social media has been its role as "an enabler for human interaction as well as an avenue to connect with other users" (Aichner et al., 2021: 219). The significance of "user-generated content," absent in its early definitions, has emerged as a central element in recent conceptualizations (p. 220). For this Element, I adopt Carr and Hayes' (2015: 50) definition, characterizing social media as "[i]nternet-based channels that allow users to interact opportunistically and selectively self-present, either in real-time or asynchronously, with both broad and narrow audiences who derive value from user-generated content and the perception of interaction with others."

Across various academic fields, the importance of the interplay between politics and social media is widely recognized. However, a notable constraint within the existing body of literature is the considerable overemphasis on studies concentrated on these dynamics within the United States, with a similar trend in other major developed nations, such as the United Kingdom. Despite some efforts to investigate these dynamics in diverse geopolitical contexts, notably around dramatic political events such as the Arab Spring, research outside Western settings remains less influential. The attempt to extrapolate insights from Western nations to varied local contexts is often impeded by significant idiosyncrasies within each region's distinct political and media systems. Consequently, understanding and findings unearthed from these contexts may have limited relevance and applicability elsewhere, including Southeast Asia.

Echoing Sinpeng and Tapsell (2020: 6), I concur that no other region undergoes the dual impact of fortune and misfortune from social media as distinctly as Southeast Asia. The region has witnessed the integration of social media platforms in significant democratic events, such as the extensive and prolonged pro-democracy youth protests in 2021 (see Section 4.4), alongside autocratic utilization of the platforms in orchestrated disinformation campaigns (see Section 5.3.2). As detailed in Section 2, Southeast Asia is one of the most socially active regions globally on various social media platforms. Furthermore, Southeast Asia is home to a wide array of political structures, cultural systems, depths of political engagement, and histories. This complex tapestry defies easy alignment with the historical timelines or categories typically employed in assessing political change within Western settings. The unique assemblages of forces at play underscore dramatically different political configurations among the nation-states of this region. It is, therefore, imperative to produce knowledge and critical insights that emerge from the empirical contexts of the region.

Over the past decade, there has been a surge of research exploring the intersection of social media and politics in Southeast Asia. This growth is particularly notable in individual case studies within specific countries. Scholars have delved into the influence of social media on diverse facets such as citizen participation, online activism, elections, state propaganda, and digital authoritarianism. The existing literature heavily focuses on Indonesia (Beta & Neyazi, 2022; Hui, 2020; Lim, 2013, 2017a; Leiliyanti & Irawati, 2020; Rakhmani & Saraswati, 2021; Saraswati, 2020; Seto, 2017; Tapsell, 2017), Malaysia (Cheong, 2020; Johns & Cheong, 2019, 2021; Lim, 2016, 2017b; Lim, 2017; Tye et al., 2018), and the Philippines (Arugay & Baquisal, 2022; Chua & Soriano, 2020; Ong & Cabañes, 2018; Ong, Tapsell, & Curato, 2019). Comparative studies of the region frequently revolve around these nations (Ong & Tapsell, 2022; Schäfer, 2018; Tapsell, 2021; Weiss, 2014). In contrast, there is a comparatively limited body of research on Myanmar (Aung & Htut, 2019; Kyaw, 2020; Passeri, 2019; Rio, 2021; Ryan & Tran, 2022), Thailand (Chattharakul, 2019; Sinpeng, 2021a, 2021b; Sombatpoonsiri, 2018, 2022), Singapore (Pang, 2020; Zhang, 2016), and Vietnam (Luong, 2020; Vu, 2017), with even less attention given to Cambodia (Doyle, 2021; Vong & Sinpeng, 2020), Laos, Timor-Leste, and Brunei. Meanwhile, regional analyses remain scarce (exceptions see Abbott, 2011; Bünte, 2020; Lim, 2019, 2023b; Sinpeng, 2020; Sinpeng & Tapsell, 2020).

In this Element, I aim to contribute to, enhance, and broaden the research within this field by exploring the dialectic relationship and assessing how this interplay played out in political communication, citizen engagement, grassroots activism, political campaigns, and elections. Building upon existing literature, which encompasses the works of Southeast Asian scholars mentioned earlier and beyond, my analysis is also rooted in my longitudinal research and observation of countries in the region.

Utilizing an interdisciplinary approach, I ground my theoretical and analytical contributions on two primary sources. First, I draw on the empirical material from my unpublished research on recent grassroots progressive and regressive activism, political campaigns, and electoral politics (primarily from 2018 to 2023). Second, I incorporate analytical and empirical insights from my past work on social media and activism in the region (Lim, 2019, 2023b), including in-depth research on Indonesia and Malaysia (Lim, 2013, 2016, 2017a, 2017b), and algorithmic dynamics (Lim, 2020a, 2023a). Bringing these together, I offer a fresh analysis with a series of arguments that evolve from and intercede with the prevailing discourse. I specifically address three critical domains of literature that predominantly influence academic discussions on social media and politics: network society and democracy (Section 1.1), social media and public spheres (Section 1.2), and, more recently, polarization and disinformation (Section 1.3). Situating my empirical research in Southeast Asia, I position the region not only as a research site but also as a source of conceptual and theoretical interventions that may find relevance elsewhere, notably in the Global South.

The principal framework of my arguments is that the relationship between social media and politics is multifaceted and co-constituting, shaped by dynamic and ever-changing technological, sociopolitical, and user contextual arrangements. In this milieu, first, I argue that the rich-gets-richer tendency of social media *scale-free* networks (Section 1.1) contributes to inequality and consolidation of power. In Southeast Asia, this means that in parallel with the exponential growth of digital networks in the last two decades, the governments, as the region's most powerful entities, have also grown to become the strongest hubs within the networks with increased capacity to control and influence political trajectories. Second, I assert that social media embodies the *platform capitalism* model rather than fostering the democratic public sphere (Section 1.2). Political pursuits on social media are thus intertwined with *communicative capitalism* (Section 1.2), where *algorithmic marketing culture* (Section 1.3) takes precedence over civic discourse and engagement. However,

Southeast Asian cases of grassroots activism show that activists and citizens have the *agency* to shape the outcomes of their social media activities while continue negotiating their positions vis-à-vis algorithmic and marketing predispositions. Lastly, I argue that, in Southeast Asia, the ascent of *algorithmic politics* (Section 1.3), employed by political actors with undemocratic motives, is the principal factor in deepening polarization and escalating disinformation, furthering autocratizing trends.

1.1 Network Society versus Democracy

Scholarly works on the intersection of digital media and politics, from early studies of the static internet to more contemporary analyses of social media, revolve mainly around the idea that network society and democracy mutually reinforce each other. While works in this area are abundant, Manuel Castells stands out as the foremost authority, evident in his *The Information Age: Economy, Society, and Culture* trilogy (1996, 1997, 1998). In these volumes, Castells explores how the rise of information and communication technologies has led to significant societal shifts, emphasizing the crucial role of networks in shaping modern social, economic, and political structures. He argues that networks have replaced traditional hierarchies as the primary organizing principle in society. Castells contends that digital communication technologies enable these networks to reconfigure political power dynamics, potentially fostering democratization through increased citizen participation and the emergence of networked social movements. However, he acknowledges that access inequality may hinder democratization by creating political engagement and influence disparities.

I contend that access inequality aside, digital networks are not egalitarian networks where citizens have equal opportunities to participate in public discourse. First and foremost, the internet is never inherently egalitarian. Instead, the internet structure exhibits characteristics of a *scale-free* network, a network whose degree distribution follows a power law (Barabási & Albert, 1999). This structure arises from two mechanisms – growth and preferential attachment – where new nodes are inclined to link with existing highly connected nodes, which are more likely to eventually become hubs (Barabási & Bonabeau, 2003).

Matthew Hindman's research (2008, 2018) supports this preferential attachment thesis. Analyzing millions of web pages, Hindman (2008) discovered that elites exert significant control over the presentation and accessibility of political content online. In his subsequent study, Hindman (2018) challenges expectations of audience fragmentation and resistance to media monopolies, asserting that giants like Google and Facebook, along with super users, dominate social media platforms. In this environment, it is mathematically impossible for smaller players to effectively compete with the elites, aligning with the *scale-free* theory.

Scale-free networks, including the internet and social media, evolve through growth and preferential attachment processes, resulting in a growing rich-get-richer phenomenon and an increasingly unequal distribution of connectivity. In social media networks, highly connected hubs hold disproportionate influence. Extreme inequality in these platforms stems from this structure, where a small number of hubs significantly impact overall network dynamics, posing challenges to democratization.

As of 2024, contemporary social media networks are more unequal than their earlier versions. In the intersection of social media and politics, these networks amplify the influence of larger political entities, reinforcing power dynamics. The ongoing growth of social media networks further enhances the dominance of powerful entities, contributing to the accumulation of power over time by those initially lacking control during the internet's early stages, such as Southeast Asian governments, including authoritarian regimes (see Section 2.3). In the region, the governments presently stand among the strongest nodes within social media's *scale-free* networks.

1.2 Social Media and Public Spheres

Another persistent focal point within the exploration of digital technologies and politics is the concept of the public sphere, drawing from the enduring Habermasian idea. Habermas (1989) envisions the public sphere as a discursive space where citizens engage in open, deliberative discourse, shaping public opinion and political decisions. The functioning public sphere comprises communicative spaces facilitating the exchange of information, ideas, and debates involving traditional mass media and contemporary digital platforms. Habermas (1989) identifies three forms of power within the public sphere – political, economic, and media power – each should adhere to the communicative rationality of presenting facts and arguments for critical scrutiny.

In examining modern democratic practices, Habermas highlights participation decline and growing disillusionment but remains optimistic about achieving a *real participatory democracy* under the *right conditions*. Despite the criticism of the notion of a rational deliberative public sphere, perceived as originating from a specific hegemonic perspective with "significant exclusions" (Fraser, 1990), the concept endures. Throughout history, from the telegraph to the internet and social media, there has been a search for media embodying these *right conditions*, prompting ongoing assessments of their potential to fulfill the requirements for a public sphere.

Early scholarly explorations of social media and the public sphere are numerous, and within this context, I draw attention to several prominent contributions. Benkler (2006) introduces the concept of a *networked public sphere*, suggesting that citizens in the networked information economy can transform their relationship with the public sphere by becoming creators and primary subjects, thus contributing to the democratization of the internet. Papacharissi (2009), recognizing both positive and negative technological effects, offers the term *virtual sphere 2.0* to describe activities such as sharing political opinions on blogs, engaging with content on YouTube, and participating in online discussion groups as manifestations of digital public spheres for citizen-consumers. Burgess and Green (2009) argue that YouTube serves as a *cultural public sphere,* facilitating encounters with cultural differences and fostering political *listening* across belief systems and identities.

Fuchs (2014) critiques these perspectives, advocating for a cultural materialist understanding of the concept grounded in political economy. He raises concerns about the ownership and commercialization of these platforms, asserting that corporate control may distort the democratic potential of the public sphere. Meanwhile, Dean (2009) disputes that the internet, rather than fostering a genuinely democratic public sphere, is integrated into the capitalist system, functioning as a tool for disseminating and promoting consumer culture. Using *communicative capitalism* to describe the fusion of communication technologies with capitalist logic, Dean argues that digital platforms can reinforce capitalist structures and influence the nature of public discourse in contemporary societies.

In recent scholarly discussions, alternative perspectives have emerged. One viewpoint argues that the promise of a digital public sphere has been hindered by autocratic challenges, with social media transitioning from an engine of protest to a potential mechanism for authoritarian resilience. It gained traction around 2016, fueled primarily by the Cambridge Analytica scandal involving the misuse of Facebook data to influence voters, notably aiding the US Trump election and the UK pro-Brexit campaign. Critics characterize this period as an era of *disinformation order* (Bennett & Livingstone, 2018) or *information disorders* (Schirch, 2021), an *epistemic crisis* (Benkler, Faris & Roberts, 2018), and *post-truth politics* (Suiter, 2016). This view aligns with the prevailing perception that digital media has become autocratic, transforming social media from a diverse landscape of liberal freedoms to a troubling domain fraught with antidemocratic threats. While this narrative of technological pessimism captures certain crucial aspects, it paints a somewhat simplified narrative that portrays social media as a distinct realm with certain features that exacerbate real-world politics.

Another viewpoint acknowledges social media's role in facilitating authoritarianism while recognizing its potential contribution to the evolution of public spheres. In contrast to the early utopian nternet scholars, proponents of this perspective do not perceive platforms as tools for democracy. Instead, scholars recognize the dual nature of technology, capable of aiding both democratization and autocratization (Schleffer & Miller, 2021; Sinpeng & Tapsell, 2020).

My perspective broadly aligns with the latter viewpoint. Drawing from my early research on the intersection of the internet and politics (Lim, 2002, 2005) to my most recent works on social media activism (Lim, 2017a, 2023a, 2023b), I acknowledge the potential for both democratic and undemocratic practices facilitated by digital platforms. Empirical cases from diverse Southeast Asian contexts reveal a historical pattern where social media platforms and their predecessors, such as the static internet, were utilized by both civil and uncivil society actors, including extremist and violent groups, pursuing progressive and regressive interests (Bräuchler, 2003; Lim, 2005; Ong & Cabañes, 2018; Sinpeng, 2021b).

It is important to recognize that the dialectical relationship between technology and politics goes beyond a simplistic attribution to the mirroring of real politics or the conventional double-edged sword argument for technology. Here, I advocate for an examination of the inherent nature of the platforms themselves. Building upon Fuchs' (2014) and Dean's (2009) ideas, I assert that social media platforms were not inherently designed for political purposes. Their inception did not prioritize fostering reasoned communicative discourse and civic engagement. Instead, social media platforms fundamentally align with what Srnicek (2017) terms *platform capitalism*. This concept delineates a specific economic and organizational model where digital platforms serve as intermediaries, connecting various user groups – consumers, producers, and advertisers – within a digital ecosystem (Srnicek, 2017).

At the heart of *platform capitalism* lies the acquisition and monetization of user data. These platforms amass extensive information about user behaviors, preferences, and interactions, utilizing data for targeted advertising to generate revenue. Moreover, *platform capitalism* thrives on network effects, where a platform's value increases with more users, creating a self-reinforcing cycle. The ultimate goal of platform capitalists is to continually increase dominance in various markets, making global connectivity an imperative objective. To maximize its performance, automation and algorithmic decision-making have thus been integrated into *platform capitalism*, influencing content recommendation, user targeting, and overall platform functionality.

Social media are the epitome of the *platform capitalism* model. They function with a proclivity toward marketing culture, treating users more as consumers than citizens. I do not imply that social media are inherently detrimental to democracy or incapable of fostering citizen participation. Social media are neither simply a sociopolitical nor a marketing artifact, but both at the same time. The commercialized marketing framework shapes users' activities but does not hold absolute power over them. Users are not simply passive subjects who have no agency; they, too, can extend and exercise their communicative agency on social media platforms as citizens. However, I underscore that any political activities on social media, including citizen and grassroots activism (see Section 4) as well as political campaigns and elections (see Section 5), are intertwined with *communicative capitalism*, wherein marketing logic takes precedence over the communicative discourse of the public spheres. Political dynamics on these platforms are shaped by attention, visibility, and information flow, aligning more with market dynamics than traditional democratic discourse (Lim, 2023a).

1.3 Social Media Algorithms, Polarization, and Disinformation

Amidst ongoing concerns about the autocratization of social media (see Section 1.1), there is a growing body of scholarship that explores three inter-related factors believed to impact democracy negatively: social media, political polarization, and the widespread dissemination of disinformation. Here, disinformation refers to information that can create misconceptions about the actual state of the world. Central to these concerns is the widespread hypothesis that social media platforms generate *filter bubbles* (Pariser, 2011), segregating users into ideological *echo chambers* (Sunstein, 2018). Some scholars emphasize the role of social media's *echo chambers* and *filter bubbles* in fostering hate speech, amplifying disinformation, deepening polarization, and enabling the rise of extreme populist communities (Govil & Baishya, 2018; Spohr, 2017; Sunstein, 2018).

In response, while recognizing the role of the platforms, some scholars believe that the perceived impact of *filter bubbles* and *echo chambers* may be overstated and contend that user information-seeking behaviors should be considered (Dubois & Blank, 2018; Zuiderveen Borgesius et al., 2016). Observably, social media users in Southeast Asia, notably in Indonesia, Malaysia, and the Philippines typically have an extensive and diverse network and are not clustered ideologically. Polarization in these places is primarily affective, not ideological.

My previous research, focusing on the interplay between algorithms, information exchanges, and social media users, demonstrated that the effect of social media interactions on users hinges on the convergence of complex forces (Lim, 2020a). In essence, the surge of disinformation and the deepening division and polarization are not causally linked to social media but are correlated. This correlation goes beyond algorithms creating isolated bubbles. Instead, as discussed in the following texts, the impact is primarily rooted in biases within three factors: *algorithmic marketing culture*, emphasizing the need for social media algorithms to support targeted advertising; the restriction of political choices through binary politics, leading to the formation of *algorithmic enclaves* (Lim, 2020a); and the escalation of *algorithmic politics* (Lim, 2023b), characterized by the professionalization of social media campaigns and the manipulation of public discourse.

Over the past decade, social media platforms have shifted from a landscape without automated content-filtering algorithms to an increasingly algorithmic environment. In this new *algorithmic culture*, ways in cultural practices and experiences are increasingly shaped by algorithms (Striphas, 2015: 395). According to Striphas (2015: 406), rather than relying on the authority of culture, algorithmic culture depends on *crowd wisdom* as the source of recommendation practices. Here, algorithmic practices and operations help the crowd by determining the "most," such as the "trending topics," "the most relevant," or the "most liked."

Contrary to the notion of serving users or achieving *crowd wisdom*, I interject that the fundamental design principle of social media algorithms primarily revolves around revenue generation through targeted advertising. Such a principle aligns with the inherent *platform capitalism* model of social media platforms, adhering to the principles of marketing culture.

Hence, I introduce the term *algorithmic marketing culture* as a conceptual framework to elucidate the interdependent interplay between algorithmic operations and marketing principles that authoritatively shape the circulation, visibility, and popularity of content among social media users. At its core is branding, which encompasses a product's symbolic value and psychological representation, where attaining virality is the ultimate marketing goal (Holt, 2016). Here, algorithms make no distinction between content produced and circulated by commercial brands and ordinary users. The visibility, popularity, and virality of user-generated content, including political content, depend not on its inherent quality but rather on its performance as a brand (Lim, 2023a). In marketing, a brand's success relies heavily on the potency of affect. Affect is the prevailing currency in the social media communication network (Lim, 2020a). The dynamics of viral communication hinge on users being adequately stirred to share and reshare content, with research indicating a preference for content eliciting high-arousal emotions like joy, excitement, anxiety, and anger (Milkman & Berger, 2012). Essentially, the bias of the *algorithmic marketing culture* leans toward content that appeals to extreme affect.

While *algorithmic marketing culture* contributes to polarization in the social media landscape, it is not the sole factor. Algorithmic recommendation and ranking systems shape online communities but do not dictate users' choices (Lim, 2020a). I argue that users are not helplessly caught in *echo chambers* and victimized by the limited exposure. Instead, users have agency. Thus, the emergence of polarized communities on social media cannot be solely attributed to algorithms; human users and the sociopolitical contexts surrounding them also play significant roles in shaping this phenomenon.

To capture the dynamic interplay between algorithms and social media users, I introduced *algorithmic enclaves*, namely: "discursive arenas where individuals, shaped by constant interactions with algorithms, engage with each other and unite based on a perceived shared identity online to defend their beliefs and safeguard their resources, often against a common enemy" (Lim, 2020a: 194). Members voluntarily shape these enclaves through their agency, coalesce around their hashtags, performing their exclusive hashtag politics.[1] These enclaves maintain a perpetual self-reinforcing loop, aiming to sustain current users and attract potential future users through repetitive processes. Given their ability to reinforce one another across platforms – the same user can trigger an algorithmic response on Instagram based on their post on Facebook post – these enclaves can become hubs for disseminating problematic message content. In other words, the algorithmic network can amplify and propagate disinformation (Lim, 2020a).

Beyond what transpires techno-socially on social media, in the last decade, we also witnessed the incorporation of *algorithmic politics*, namely, politics that revolves around the algorithmic manipulation of issues, primarily aimed at dominating media spheres to influence public opinion (Lim, 2023b: 39). *Algorithmic politics* encompasses a range of political maneuvers that leverage existing algorithmic biases to influence the public. In Southeast Asia, it becomes prominent when political actors exploit algorithms to sway citizens' decisions during elections and everyday political matters. Hence, I contend that the utilization of *algorithmic politics* by political actors plays an essential role in undermining democracy and contributing to the autocratization trend in the region.

1.4 Structure of This Element

This Element is organized as follows:

> Section 1 situates my contribution within existing debates and literature, presenting the analytical framework rooted in three key domains: network society and democracy, social media, and public spheres, and recent concerns about polarization and disinformation.

---

[1] Hashtag politics refers to the use of hashtags on social media platforms as a strategic tool for political communication, activism, or engagement. It involves creating and popularizing specific hashtags to promote, discuss, organize, and/or mobilize around shared political issues/topics, events, or campaigns on social media platforms.

Section 2 delves into the state of social media in the region, providing a sociopolitical and technological background for the analysis. It situates the nexus of social media and politics in three contextual factors: the emergence of Southeast Asia as the social media marketplace, the intertwining of politics in social and personal spheres, and the increased governments' control and autocratic tendencies.

Section 3 offers a panoramic view of social media and politics in Southeast Asia. Examining each nation, it provides a regional overview of diverse approaches and levels of digital freedom and states' control, chronicling the platforms' employment for mobilization, activism, campaigns, and disinformation dissemination.

Section 4 explores how activists and citizens in Southeast Asia take advantage of social media *affordances*, contributing to heightened grassroots activism, presenting insights from diverse country cases, and discussing the binary and affective nature of activism.

Section 5 empirically and analytically examines the role of social media platforms in political communication, campaigns, and electoral politics. It discusses the utilization of *algorithmic politics* for manipulating the public, disseminating disinformation, and deepening polarization.

Section 6 is offers a reflective summary of the comprehensive analysis discussed throughout this Element. It encapsulates the key findings and insights derived from exploring the intricate relationship between social media and politics in Southeast Asia.

2 Mapping the Terrain: Sociopolitical and Technological Dynamics of Social Media in Southeast Asia

The internet entered parts of Southeast Asia in the 1980s, primarily through research institutions and university networks. However, its widespread availability only commenced in the mid 1990s with the advent of commercial and public internet service providers all over the region. Due to its economic potential, governments in the region enthusiastically embraced the technology and made significant investments in internet infrastructure. Malaysia established the Multimedia Super Corridor, an advanced business center to propel the country into the information society. Singapore invested billions in its internet infrastructure to create an "intelligent island." Indonesia formulated a national internet development plan named *Visi Nusantara-21* (Vision of the Twenty-First-Century Archipelago), drawing inspiration from the US National Information Infrastructure. Other countries followed suit, prioritizing the internet as a crucial element of national development plans.

In the early 2000s, the internet penetration in Southeast Asia was very low, with only Singapore and Malaysia having more than 10 percent of their online population (Lim, 2023b). However, over two decades, the growth has been exponential (Figure 1). In 2023, 75.6 percent of the 684 million people residing in Southeast Asia were internet users, surpassing the global average of 64.4 percent. In Brunei, Malaysia, and Singapore, over 90 percent of the population was online; Myanmar and Timor-Leste were the least-wired countries, with 44 percent and 49 percent (Table 1).

In contrast to the initial phases of internet development in the 2000s, where the online population was predominantly urban (Lim, 2019), there is now a weaker correlation between a country's urbanization rate and its corresponding percentage of online users (Table 1). This shift is attributed to the widespread use of mobile phones for internet connectivity in Southeast Asia (Table 1, Figure 2). The ease of establishing wireless technology hubs and the growing availability of affordable mobile devices fueled the significant expansion of technology adoption beyond large urban centers. In 2023, except for Laos, all countries had more mobile phones than people, with Vietnam leading with 164 percent.

During the initial internet development period in the mid 1990s, governments focused on expanding access through telephone-based internet connections and broadband infrastructure expansion. However, the increasing popularity of mobile phones led to the abandonment of telephone development, evident in the steady decline of telephone line subscribers in nearly all countries (Figure 3). Vietnam, which aggressively built its telephony infrastructure in 2003, experienced a decline in 2009. Cambodia started the development in 2009, only to halt it in 2012. In 2022, Brunei and Malaysia were the only countries expanding their fixed telephony infrastructure. Fixed (wired)-broadband subscriptions have remained relatively low, with all countries except Singapore having fewer than 25 subscriptions per 100 people (Figure 4). The sluggish progress in broadband infrastructure development and the prohibitive cost of broadband subscriptions contributed to the shift toward mobile internet, driving its exponential growth. In simpler terms, the significant growth of smartphones played a significant role in driving the substantial expansion of the online population in the region. Consequently, this propelled the exponential growth of social media users in Southeast Asia, given that most users access these platforms through mobile devices (mobile social media) (Table 1).

In 2021, the Philippines led the global rankings, with its users spending an astonishing close to eleven hours a day online. By 2023, the Philippines had slipped to the third position, logging 9:14 hours of daily online activity. Even with this slight decline in ranking, Southeast Asian users continued to outpace

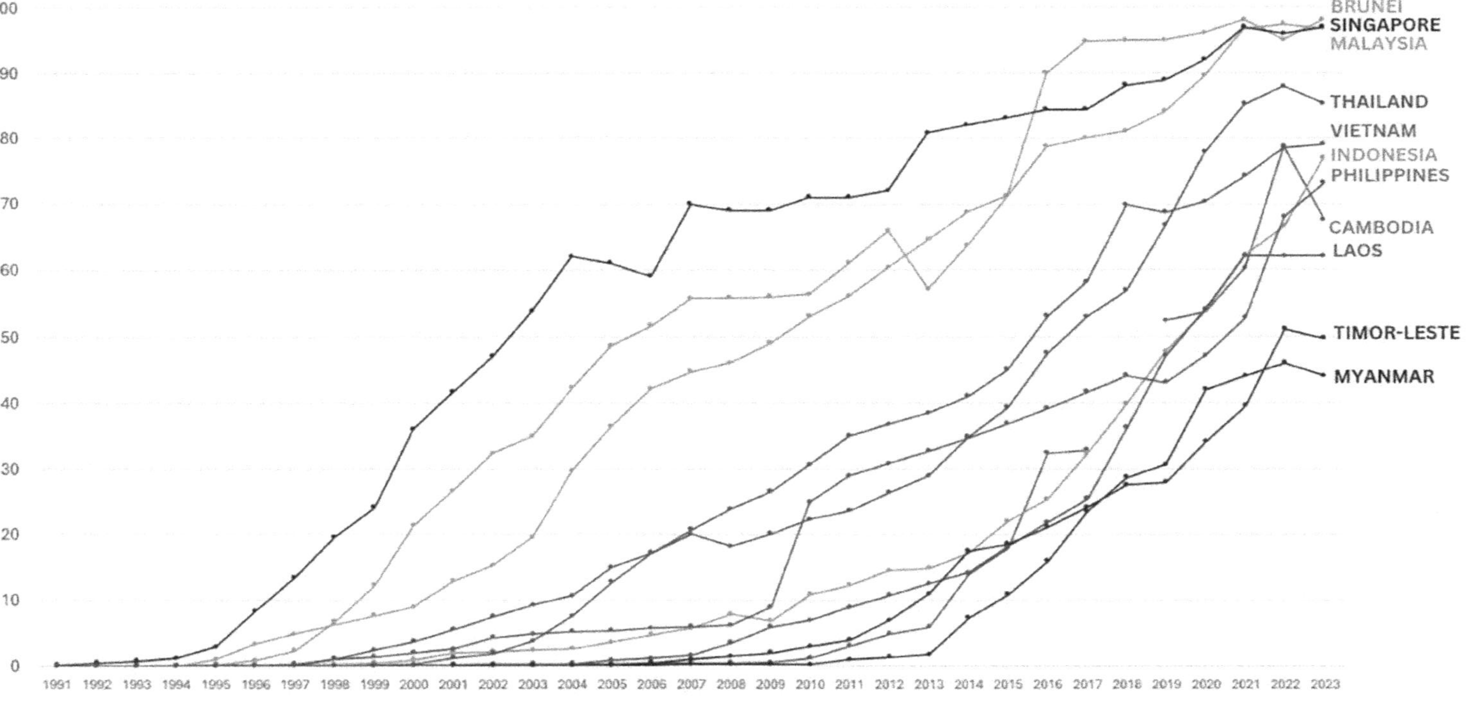

Figure 1 The internet users (percent) in Southeast Asia (1991–2023)

Source: Author, based on World Bank (2024) and Data Reportal (2023b).

Table 1 The internet, mobile, and social media shares in Southeast Asia (2023)[2]

Country	Total population (million)	Urban	Literacy (15+)	internet (18+)	Mobile phones	Mobile internet	Social media	Social media	Mobile social media (18+)
Brunei	0.4508	79.00%	97.20%	98.10%	127.80%	96.14%	94.40%	120.60%	118.19%
Cambodia	16.86	25.30%	80.50%	67.50%	131.50%	66.89%	65.00%	88.00%	87.21%
Indonesia	276.40	58.20%	96.00%	77.00%	128.00%	75.69%	60.40%	79.50%	78.15%
Laos	7.58	37.90%	84.70%	62.00%	85.10%	62.00%	44.20%	61.10%	61.10%
Malaysia	34.13	78.40%	95.00%	96.80%	129.10%	92.06%	78.50%	99.80%	94.91%
Myanmar	54.38	32.00%	89.10%	44.00%	118.80%	44.00%	27.60%	36.60%	36.60%
The Philippines	116.50	48.20%	95.30%	73.10%	144.50%	71.13%	72.50%	102.40%	99.64%
Singapore	6.00	100.00%	97.10%	96.90%	153.80%	86.73%	84.70%	89.30%	79.92%
Thailand	71.75	53.20%	93.80%	85.30%	141.00%	81.29%	72.80%	84.80%	80.81%
Timor-Leste	1.35	32.10%	68.10%	49.60%	106.60%	49.60%	26.20%	40.00%	40.00%
Vietnam	98.53	39.10%	95.80%	79.10%	164.00%	75.54%	71.00%	89.00%	88.56%

[2] Compiled by author, data from Data Reportal (2023a, 2023b). The percentage of internet, mobile phones, social media, and mobile social media users were calculated as a percentage of total population.

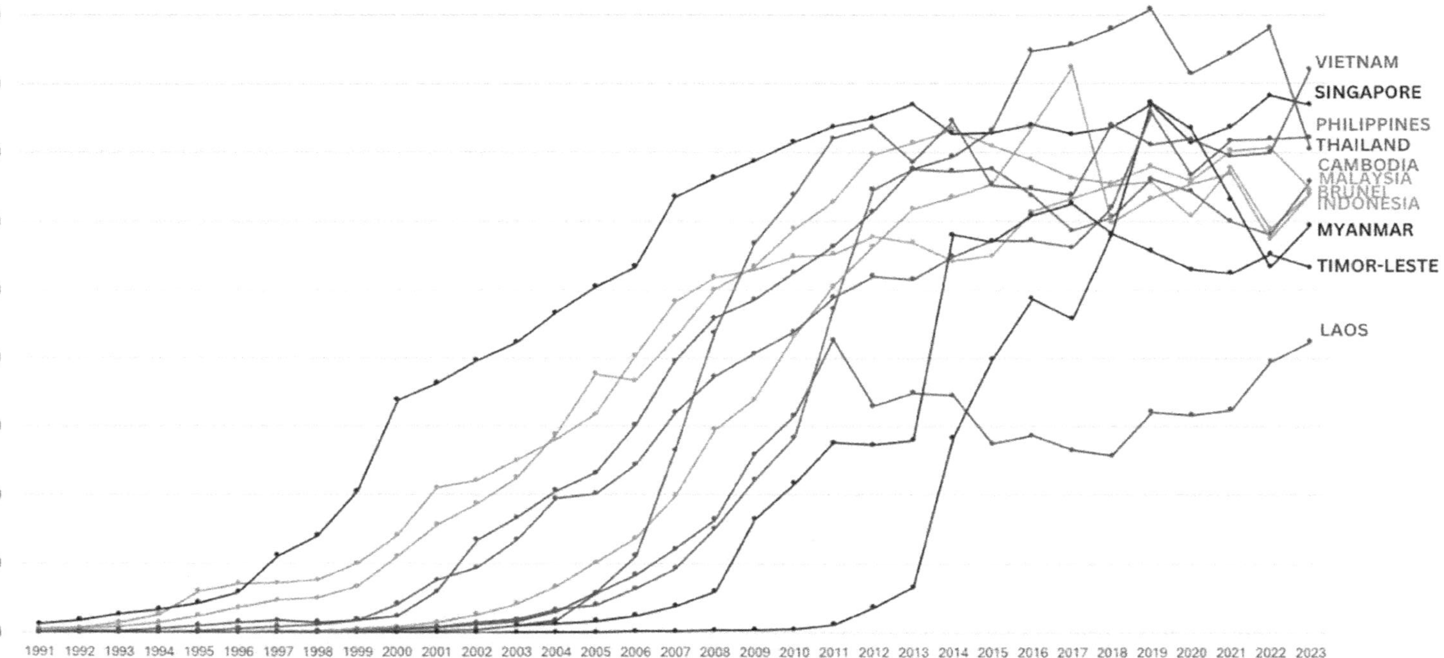

Figure 2 Mobile phone users (percent) in Southeast Asia (1991–2023)

Source: Author, based on World Bank (2024) and Data Reportal (2023b).

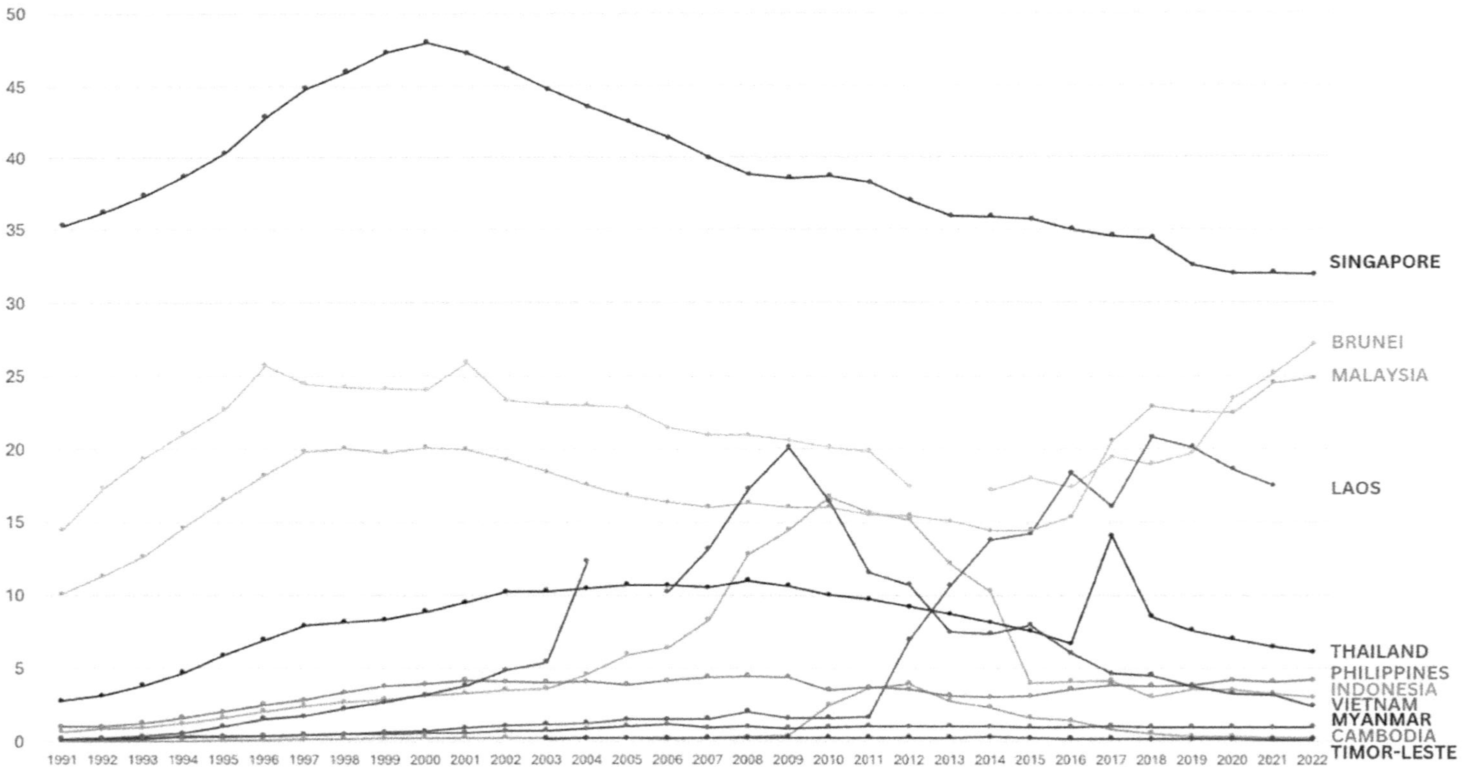

Figure 3 Fixed telephone subscriptions (per 100 people) in Southeast Asia (1991–2022)

Source: Author, based on World Bank (2024).

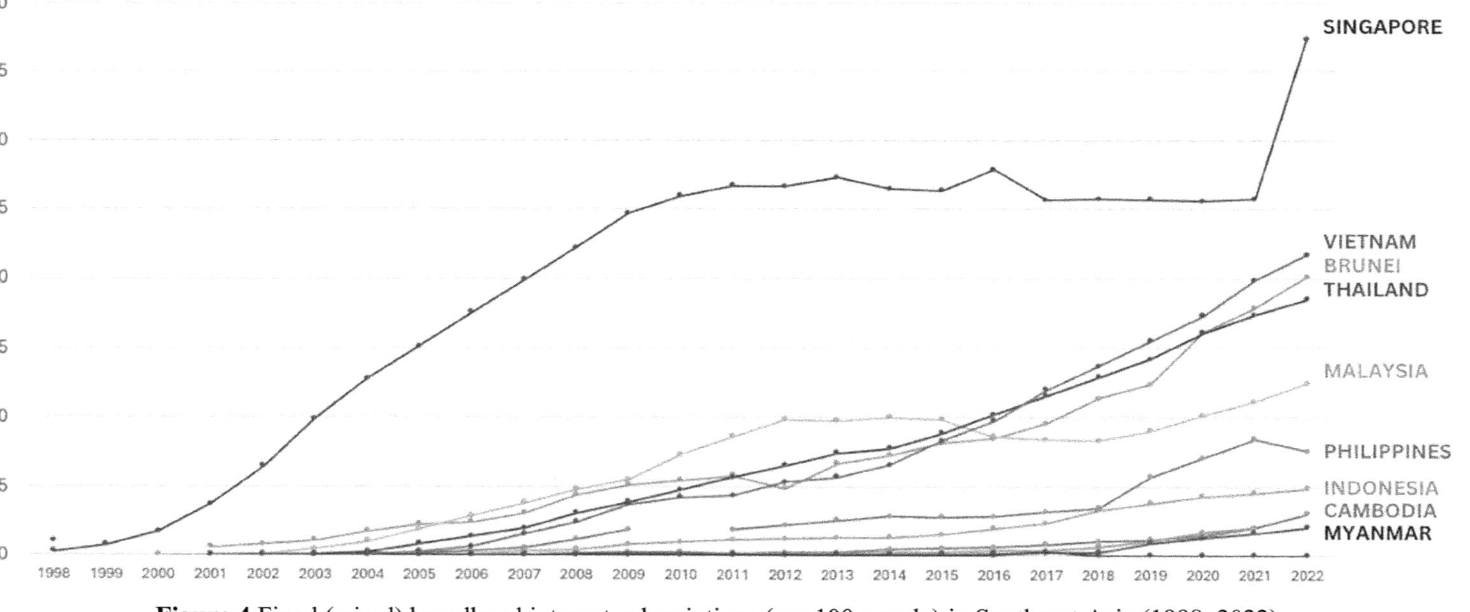

Figure 4 Fixed (wired) broadband internet subscriptions (per 100 people) in Southeast Asia (1998–2022)

Source: Author, based on World Bank (2024).

the global average for time spent online, at 6:37 hours, highlighting the region's sustained high level of digital connectivity and interaction. Ranked within the top thirty globally, Malaysia clocked in at 8:07, Thailand at 8:06, Indonesia at 7:42, Singapore at 06:42, and Vietnam at 06:23 (Data Reportal, 2023a).

However, despite these impressive figures, in 2023, there were still 166.7 million individuals who remained unconnected. It is also crucial to highlight that despite the overall high population in the region, there exist disparities in usage. Technologically, there is a noticeable discrepancy in connection speeds among and within countries. While Bruneians enjoyed a swift 102.06 Mbps (megabytes per second) in median download speeds for mobile internet connection and Singaporeans experienced 72.18 Mbps, users in other Southeast Asian countries faced slower connections, ranging from 17.27 Mbps in Indonesia to 39.59 Mbps in Vietnam (Data Reportal, 2023a).

The majority of the Southeast Asian population, 63.7 percent, was active on social media, exceeding the global average of 59.4 percent (Data Reportal, 2023a). Facebook has maintained its status as the predominant platform in the region over an extended period (Table 2), primarily because it has been tailored to function on low-end feature phones that are widespread in economically challenged areas of the region. However, Facebook and Twitter have encountered slight declines in user numbers across various countries. In recent years, TikTok emerged as a platform experiencing exponential growth in usage. In Malaysia, TikTok's popularity has exceeded Facebook's (Table 2). In just one year, from 2022 to 2023, the number of TikTok users in Southeast Asia has doubled. Notably, Indonesia, Malaysia, Singapore, the Philippines, Thailand, and Vietnam collectively represented about half of the platform's user population in the Asia Pacific, excluding China. For young people, particularly Gen Z, TikTok also functions as a search engine, substituting Google (Huang, 2022). Simultaneously, WhatsApp has established a robust regional presence (Table 2). Social media users in Indonesia, Malaysia, and Singapore overwhelmingly cited WhatsApp as their favorite platform (Data Reportal, 2023a). Beyond platforms cited in Table 2, Telegram was popular in Indonesia, Malaysia, and Thailand, Zalo in Vietnam, and Line in Thailand. Meanwhile, in recent years, Signal reportedly started gaining popularity among activists due to its safety and privacy protection; Signal conversations are end-to-end encrypted.

With the widespread and intense adoption of social media now considered the norm, these platforms have assumed a pivotal role in citizens' daily lives, exerting influence across realms such as work, family, entertainment, and politics. Integrating social media into political dynamics is anything but a static scenario with a predetermined outcome, be it democratization, polarization, or autocratization. The results exhibit a nuanced spectrum with diverse

Table 2 Social media platforms' shares in Southeast Asia (2023)[3]

Country	Facebook	YouTube	Twitter	Instagram	Messenger	Tiktok	WhatsApp
Brunei	71.10%		27.00%	74.10%	40.40%		45.94%
Cambodia	82.60%		3.10%	13.80%	56.90%	63.70%	33.21%
Indonesia	55.40%	55.10%	11.10%	41.20%	12.60%	56.80%	40.52%
Laos	57.40%		4.30%	8.90%	41.30%		17.15%
Malaysia	73.80%	79.80%	20.00%	50.70%	40.80%	77.70%	66.22%
Myanmar	33.9%%			3.30%	26.40%		35.31%
The Philippines	95.50%	61.60%	13.70%	20.40%	60.50%	58.20%	75.54%
Singapore	61.30%	86.00%	103.00%	50.10%	36.20%	46.50%	76.67%
Thailand	77.10%	54.30%	23.40%	27.80%	56.20%	69.10%	40.98%
Timor-Leste	36.50%		0.80%	7.00%	7.60%		21.98%
Vietnam	83.40%	68.90%	5.20%	13.00%	66.30%	68.90%	30.24%

[3] Compiled by author, data from Data Reportal (2023a, 2023b) and World Population Review (2023). Facebook's, YouTube's, Twitter's, and Instagram's shares of audience were calculated based on potential advertising audience compared to the total population aged 13+; Tiktok aged 18+. WhatsApps' shares of users were calculated based on their percentage of the total online population.

outcomes (see Sections 4 and 5), transcending a simplistic dichotomy of users as either "good guys" utilizing it positively or "bad guys" engaging negatively.

Furthermore, in Southeast Asia, politics takes place within a context fashioned by three contextual factors. First, political endeavors are shaped by marketing propensity as Southeast Asia emerges as the social media marketplace for consumers and corporations. Second, citizens engage with politics on social media, integrating political discourse into the fabric of social and personal aspects. Lastly, the politics of social media dynamically align with changing political contexts, especially concerning state control, repression, and autocratizing tendencies in the regional political landscape.

2.1 Southeast Asia as the Marketplace

The statistics on social media users and engagement in Southeast Asia make the region highly appealing for platform companies and advertisers, marking it the fastest-growing online market globally. According to Nielsen's report, advertising spending in Southeast Asia reached US$ 44.7 billion, growing by 12 percent annually, with a significant boost from a 64 percent increase in digital advertising in 2021 (Adnews, 2023).

Southeast Asia is regarded as a digital giant comparable to China, holding exceptional significance as a prime social media market and advertising target for several reasons. First, it boasts a vast and rapidly expanding population, constituting a dynamic market. The demographic is characterized by a predominantly youthful population dedicating approximately 60 percent of their waking hours to online activities, presenting an attractive market for brands and advertisers (Kemp, 2021).

Second, the region has witnessed remarkable digital penetration and intense social media engagement. Third, the mobile-first connectivity trend, prevalent in the region, offers advertisers a unique opportunity to engage with users in a personalized and immediate manner. Fourth, the growing e-commerce sector, with nearly $100 billion in transactions in 2022, further enhances Southeast Asia's appeal to investors and advertisers, creating a fertile environment for online shopping trends (Momentum Works, 2023). Significant investments in digital businesses are contributing to expanding platforms such as Shopee, Lazada, InMobi, and Tokopedia.

Lastly, Southeast Asian countries are recognized as emerging markets, with projections indicating the potential addition of approximately 51 million new high- and upper-middle-class households by 2030 (Bain & Company, 2022). Rising disposable incomes and evolving consumer behavior provide advertisers with favorable opportunities to establish and fortify their brand presence in these emerging economies.

Southeast Asia emerges as a dynamic and lucrative region for businesses seeking to connect with a vibrant consumer base, driving market expansion. This reality, explored further in Sections 4 and 5, has political implications driven by two key factors: the prevalence of branding to expand user bases in the social media marketplace (including the political marketplace) and the inherent influence of marketing culture on politics and political activities within social media.

2.2 Personal, Social, and Political

While this Element focuses on the intersection of social media and politics, it is crucial to note that political engagement is not the primary motivation for individuals using these platforms. In Southeast Asia, individuals aged sixteen to sixty-four mainly used social media to "keep in touch with friends and family," with "finding information" and "keeping up-to-date with news and events" being secondary and tertiary reasons (Data Reportal, 2023b). Politics becomes intertwined with these diverse activities, seamlessly unfolding as users engage in daily social and personal interactions on social media.

Political encounters and discussions are also influenced by the need to stay informed and participate in social conversations, possibly driven by the Fear of Missing Out (FOMO). "Seeing what's being talked about" was a top reason users use social media platforms (Data Reportal, 2023b).

Importantly, online and social media are overwhelmingly preferred sources of news across Southeast Asia, with over 86 percent of the population in Indonesia, Malaysia, the Philippines, Singapore, and Thailand identifying online news as their primary source and 68 percent relying on social media (Reuters Institute, 2022). The significance of television and print media has diminished, including among older audiences. In 2023, trust in news media stood at 42.6 percent, aligning closely with the global average of 40 percent. Southeast Asian countries ranked high in the percentage of adults expressing concerns about misinformation and fake news (Data Reportal, 2023b).

In social media, the personal, social, and political facets are intricately connected, contributing to the heightened personalization of politics. These platforms tailor political messages beyond politicians and parties to individual users, evident in how citizens express their political opinions, discuss political events, and form communities around specific issues. Political content coexists with other content types, such as cat photos, celebrity gossip, memes, music videos, Netflix series comments, and updates from friends' activities. For most social media users, politics is a transient yet recurring element encountered and consumed through engagement, interaction, and reactions to various political events and issues.

2.3 Control and Repression of the Autocratizing Southeast Asia

In contrast to the earlier days of the internet when digital space was relatively open, governments have significantly bolstered their capabilities to monitor and control the digital sphere. Aligned with the logic of *scale-free* networks (Section 1.1), states, as powerful actors, have exponentially increased their power within digital networks. As of 2023, the Freedom House reported that no country in Southeast Asia has "free" internet (see Table 3). For the "Freedom of the World" (political rights and civil liberties) index, Timor-Leste was cited as the only "free" country in the region, while other nations performed poorly. The region also scored low in the press freedom index, with only Timor-Leste being deemed satisfactory. Here, it is important to take the notion of "free" with caution, as a closer look at Timor-Leste reveals that it is not as free as the report suggested (see Section 3.10).

The escalating use of control and repression in the region is closely tied to the global trend of autocratization. Varieties of Democracy (V-Dem) reported that in 2023 there were more autocracies than democracies worldwide, with over 72 percent of the global population residing in autocratic regimes. The progress in global democratic levels achieved over the past thirty-five years

Table 3 Freedom in Southeast Asia (2023)[4]

Country	Freedom in the world index (score/category)	Internet freedom index (score/category)	World press freedom index (rank out of 180)
Brunei	28/Not free	–	142/Difficult
Cambodia	24/Not free	44/Partly free	147/Difficult
Indonesia	58/Partly free	47/Partly free	108/Problematic
Laos	13/Not free	–	160/Very serious
Malaysia	53/Partly free	61/Partly free	73/Problematic
Myanmar	9/Not free	10/Not free	173/Very serious
The Philippines	58/Partly free	61/Partly free	132/Difficult
Singapore	47/Partly free	54/Partly free	129/Difficult
Thailand	30/Not free	39/Not free	106/Problematic
Timor-Leste	72/Free	–	10/Satisfactory
Vietnam	19/Not free	22/Not free	178/Very serious

---

[4] Compiled by author, data from Freedom House (2023a) and RSF (2023).

has been erased, regressing to 1986. However, Southeast Asia's decline is particularly pronounced, with democratic conditions regressed to 1978 levels (V-Dem, 2023).

V-Dem (2023) identified Malaysia as the sole nation in the region undergoing a democratization process from 2012 to 2022, though in recent years, such a process has been problematic (see Section 3.5). In contrast, all other Southeast Asian countries exhibit a trajectory toward autocratization, even those already governed by authoritarian regimes. This unsettling trend permeates the spectrum, impacting nations in different democratic phases, such as Indonesia and the Philippines. Myanmar, following a military coup, transitioned from an electoral autocracy to a closed autocracy. Thailand, since the military takeover in 2014 and the subsequent severe repression, has ranked among the top ten autocratizing nations globally in the last decade.

In the social media age, Southeast Asian governments have significantly enhanced their capacity to regulate the digital landscape, employing various technical and legal tools. Across certain nations, authorities have implemented measures to control online speech, utilizing stringent laws and pressuring platform companies to censor content, deactivate accounts, and remove posts critical of the government. Major social media platforms, including Facebook, have complied with government directives to remove content violating national laws. Some governments extended existing criminal laws into the online domain, such as Indonesia's defamation law and Thailand's *lèse-majesté* law (Section 3.9). Additionally, cybersecurity and anti-fake news laws, often vaguely defining criminalizable speech, provide a pretext for increased data surveillance and crackdowns on dissent under the guise of defending cybersecurity and combating fake news (Lim, 2023b).

Virtually every country has instituted legislation addressing electronic transactions.[5] Nine out of eleven are presently enforcing cybersecurity regulations, while Laos and Timor-Leste have also presented drafts of their respective laws. Ominously, cybersecurity laws in certain countries, particularly Vietnam and Thailand, have conferred unauthorized access to private data and computer systems to the government, facilitating the suppression of dissent. In Cambodia, the September 2022 draft of the cybersecurity law allows the authorities to seize computer systems and access user data under broad circumstances linked to national security and public order. Distinct legislative measures, such as Vietnam's "Decree 72" and Laos' stringent internet law, exemplify efforts to control online content and curtail opposition voices. Meanwhile, Indonesia's

---

[5] See Poetranto, Lau, and Gold (2021) for further examination of the cybersecurity in the region, particularly Indonesia and Singapore.

Ministerial Regulation No. 5 of 2020 represents a content moderation regime threatening freedom of expression and user privacy.

The proliferation of anti-fake news laws in countries like Cambodia, Myanmar, Singapore, and Thailand has encountered criticism for allegedly suppressing dissent. After repealing a much-criticized anti-fake news law in 2018, Malaysia enacted an emergency law in early 2021 targeting fake news related to COVID-19. Vietnam also introduced a law in 2020 to counter the spread of fake news as a pandemic-related security measure. Beyond the pandemic, governments in the region persist in efforts to control content through diverse mechanisms. For instance, in December 2022, the Malaysian government established a dedicated task force to address issues of purportedly false news and "sensitive or provocative" content about the "3Rs": race, religion, and royalty.

These laws bear considerable repercussions for citizen engagement on social media, with each country reportedly initiating investigations, making arrests, or securing convictions based on these regulations. In Thailand, 164 individuals faced *lèse-majesté* charges within a year since November 2020, with 83 accused of posting critical messages about the monarchy on social media (TLHR, 2021). Vietnam has experienced a rise in "prisoners of conscience," escalating from 75 in 2013 to 128 in 2019, with around 70 serving jail terms, primarily for their activities on platforms like Facebook and YouTube (Amnesty International, 2021). Meanwhile, the Indonesian government misused the transaction law (ITE) defamation clause to criminalize journalists who exposed prominent figures' corrupt and unethical conduct. Online defamation cases in Indonesia surged from merely five in 2009–2010 to 768 in 2016–2020 (Mann, 2021). Furthermore, employing sedition laws and the Communication and Multimedia Act, Malaysia has targeted and arrested digital activists and news organizations critical of the government, leading to a "chilling effect" on free speech (Johns & Cheong, 2019).

In nations undergoing autocratization, there is a discernible increase in media censorship, repression of civil society organizations, and limitations on political freedom. The interplay of autocratization, rising disinformation, and growing polarization, notably evident on social media, reinforces each other in these nations.

3 Revealing the Tapestry: Country Highlights on Social Media and Politics in Southeast Asia

This section provides succinct narratives on the interplay between social media and politics within every Southeast Asian nation. It focuses on critical factors such as the degree of internet and social media freedom and control and unveils the diverse approaches taken by each country, revealing these platforms' implications in mobilization, activism, campaigns, and disinformation dissemination. Through the presentation of these highlights, the section aims to offer a panoramic view, unveiling the nuanced landscape of social media and politics in Southeast Asia.

Overall, the legal and regulatory landscape in the region has become more restricted, with increasing state control and surveillance in all countries. Yet, there has been a rise in grassroots politics across nearly all countries in the region, with increased integration of social media. There are some variations across different countries. Indonesia, the Philippines, and Malaysia, which witnessed historical political events incorporating the static internet, continue to be the epicenters of grassroots activism in the social media era. Authoritarian countries such as Vietnam, Cambodia, Myanmar, and postcoup Thailand have witnessed online and offline dissents. Social media activism exists in Singapore but typically does not translate into street activism. Brunei is the only country that had no activism. Meanwhile, social media has played an increasing role in political campaigns and elections and has helped new players, outsiders, and opposition gain a foothold. However, authoritarian capture has emerged, where social media is used as a tool for authoritarian resilience.

Due to the dynamic nature of both realms, providing a fresh inquiry into the intersection of social media and politics presents a complex challenge. Despite my efforts to capture key developments in each country and maintain the relevance of any overarching observations amidst ongoing political and technological transformations, I acknowledge the limitations of this endeavor. Therefore, my country-by-country analysis, which concluded by December 2023,[6] should be perceived as a blend of historical consideration and current insights aimed at illuminating, not foreseeing, conceivable future trends.

3.1 Brunei

With a GDP per capita of US$37,152, Brunei is among the world's wealthiest nations (World Bank, 2023). It is the only absolute Islamic monarchy in Southeast Asia where politics is intricately linked with the state ideology of *Melayu Islam Beraja* (Malay Islamic Monarchy). In this context, being Malay signifies being Muslim and loyal to the monarchy, shaping citizenship through adherence to Islam and allegiance to the Sultanate. A decade ago, Li (2012) observed that Bruneians' use of digital media was guided by self-restraint and respect for the royal family. This trend persists in 2023, with individuals practicing self-censorship despite active participation in relatively free social media platforms.

---

[6] Especially for Indonesia, I included selected updates around the 2024 elections.

Brunei is not a free country. For over sixty years, emergency laws have restricted freedom of assembly to groups of no more than ten people without a permit. The unicameral legislative council lacks independent political standing and functions under the Sultan's appointments. Since 1962, direct legislative elections have not taken place, and political opposition remains extremely limited, with the National Development Party (NDP) being the sole registered party since 2005 (Freedom House, 2023b).

The Sultan's family owns or controls the media, resulting in a lack of diversity and freedom. The Brunei Defamation Act and the 2005 Sedition Act further curtail freedom of expression, hindering individuals and the media from exercising freedom of speech. Newspapers can be arbitrarily closed, and journalists may face imprisonment for up to three years for reporting deemed "libel and slander" (Lim, 2019). Sharia-based criminal regulations were introduced in 2014, with a moratorium on capital punishment issued in May 2019 after a mandate for death by stoning (Freedom House, 2023b).

Despite a significant increase in the internet population from 3 percent in 2000 to over 98 percent in 2023, with nearly all adults over eighteen on social media, there is no evidence of it fostering political resistance in Brunei. Internet access, reportedly unrestricted, is provided by a state-owned ISP, and government control extends to digital content through an internet practice code (Lim, 2019). The Brunei government employs an informant system to monitor dissidents and scrutinizes online communications for subversive content. In 2019, Shahiransheriffuddin bin Shahrani Muhammad, who criticized the government's halal certification policy in a 2017 Facebook post, received an eighteen-month sentence in absentia and sought asylum in Canada due to fears of persecution for being gay (Bandial, 2019).

Amid the controlled media landscape, there exists *The Scoop*, which is an independent online news portal that supposedly is "financed primarily through advertising revenue and independent of government or political interests" (The Scoop, 2023). Established in September 2017, the platform articulates its commitment to "maintaining openness and accessibility" while concentrating on "informing and empowering Bruneians, fostering engagement with current issues, and influencing public discourse" (The Scoop, 2023). While covering various sociocultural issues, *The Scoop* maintains an apolitical tone. However, given the nature of Bruneian media, which is largely under the Sultan's control, *The Scoop*'s commitment to independence becomes notably political.

3.2 Cambodia

Since 1985, Cambodia's political system has been dominated by former prime minister Hun Sen, the father of current Premier Hun Manet, and the Cambodian

People's Party (CPP). The media landscape is marked by deep politicization stemming from a historical legacy of factionalism and political patronage (Lim, 2019). Media magnates with close ties to the Hun Sen family own and control the mass media market in Cambodia. Despite a 1995 press law encouraging amicable resolution of defamation cases, authorities frequently resort to the penal code to prosecute and apprehend journalists delving into sensitive issues, often without a warrant. Specifically, articles 494 and 495 in criminal law sections addressing "inciting crime" are invoked in such cases (Freedom House, 2023c).

In 2023, 67.50 percent of the population were online users, and 88 percent of adults over eighteen used social media. This represents a significant increase from 1 percent of internet users recorded in 2010. Even back then, despite a low internet penetration, the government was wary of the internet's political potential, particularly regarding its utilization by the opposition. To control information flow, the government designated the state-owned telephone company as the sole operator for internet exchanges, ostensibly to filter out explicit content but also to stifle criticisms against the CPP. Despite this control, the internet remained a more accessible medium than others, offering space for emerging alternative voices within certain constraints.

The late 2000s witnessed the emergence of social media in Cambodia, providing a venue for public expression and dissent often absent in traditional media characterized by self-censorship. This shift empowered political opposition groups, particularly the Cambodia National Rescue Party (CNRP), fostering increased political discourse among young, educated voters and influencing the 2013 elections (see Section 5.2.1) (Vong & Sinpeng, 2020). The online presence of the opposition expanded, resulting in street protests in Phnom Penh in January 2014, as censored accounts reached broader audiences through social media. In response, authorities escalated repression, crackdowns, and violence against civilians.

With lessons learned from 2013, Prime Minister Hun Sen launched a clampdown on independent media in 2017 in preparation for the 2018 elections. During the 2018 electoral campaigns, Hun Sen extended his influence on social media, crafting a persona while issuing conditional promises and blending threats with notions of peace (Doyle, 2021). In 2023, Hun Sen solidified his social media campaigns in a controversial election that excluded the opposition party (see Section 5.2.2). Just months before the election, Kem Sokha, the former president of CNRP, was sentenced to twenty-seven years in jail on charges of conspiring with foreign forces to overthrow the government. The ruling party won nearly all seats, and thus, Hun Sen's son, Hun Manet, assumed the position of prime minister.

Presently, repression against initiatives supporting independent journalism persists, compounded by the pro-government stance of traditional media outlets. Cambodians thus increasingly rely on online media for reliable news, leveraging the widespread availability of mobile phones. Furthermore, the government's intent to establish a Chinese-style digital Great Wall, granting authority to monitor and block sites, raises significant concerns about online freedom for Cambodians (Ratcliffe, 2022).

3.3 Indonesia

For over three decades, under the authoritarian regime of President Suharto, the country ranked among the least free in Southeast Asia, where the media was tightly controlled. In the mid 1990s, the internet became commercially available in the country. The Suharto regime did not impose regulations on the emerging online space, partially due to the novelty of the technology, making it challenging for the government to control. The economic crisis further left the internet unmanaged. Between 1996 and 1998, especially during the peak of the Asian financial crisis, the internet became a vital platform for discussing and criticizing the regime, playing an important role in activating anti-Suharto sentiment (Lim, 2002).

The fall of Suharto in 1998 brought significant changes to freedom of expression and increased access to information, leaving the internet largely unregulated. However, in recent years, internet freedom and freedom of speech have declined. Concerns persist about the politicized use of defamation and blasphemy laws and the impact of the 2008 Information and Electronic Transactions (ITE) Law on internet freedom. In 2020, Ministerial Regulation No. 5 introduced a content moderation regime that threatens freedom of expression and user privacy. Meanwhile, government critics, journalists, and internet users continue to face criminal prosecution, violent attacks, and harassment in retaliation for their online activities, especially by Papuan activists (Freedom House, 2023d). Internet access in Papua continues to be routinely disrupted (Lim, 2020b).

In 2023, 77 percent of the total population was online, and nearly 80 percent of adults over eighteen were on social media. In the last decade, digital activism continues to exist, involving a significant portion of the urban middle class, as seen in the anti-corruption movements in the late 2000s (Lim, 2013; Suwana, 2020) and pro-reform students' movements in the late 2010s (Sastramidjaja, 2020) and early 2020s (Section 4.4). While social media platforms offer space for activism across various causes, including those representing marginalized communities such as Ahmadiyyas, Shias (Schäfer, 2018), and Papuans (Kusumaryati, 2021), the media landscape tends to favor simplified narratives tailored for urban middle-class consumers. Simultaneously, it is unfavorable for complex narratives of justice, inequalities, or the poor (Lim, 2013).

Social media campaigns are central to electoral politics. In the 2012 Jakarta gubernatorial election, Joko Widodo (Jokowi) and his running mate Basuki Purnama Tjahja (Ahok) became the first candidates to rely heavily on social media campaigns. Subsequent elections, including the 2014, 2019, and 2024 presidential elections and the highly divisive 2017 Jakarta gubernatorial race, saw candidates embrace *algorithmic politics* to manipulate public opinions. Notably, Prabowo Subianto's victory in 2024 further solidified the authoritarian turn initiated in Jokowi's second term (Section 5.2.2).

Beyond elections, algorithmic dynamics continued to be part of political engagements, contributing to deepening affective polarization, segregating Indonesians into exclusionary *algorithmic enclaves* that reinforced tribal nationalism and excluded considerations of equality and justice for others (Lim, 2017a: 444).

3.4 Laos

Laos operates as a one-party state, where the ruling Lao People's Revolutionary Party (LPRP) exerts control over all facets of politics and imposes strict limitations on civil liberties. There is an absence of organized opposition, independent civil society, or a free and independent media sector. In 2001, the Laotian government undertook a groundbreaking domestic media reform by introducing the new Mass Media Bill, allowing for the establishment of private media enterprises. This marked a departure from the established model of journalists as government officials tasked with unifying the party, state, and masses. However, private owners are mandated to pledge loyalty to the party's principles, and any reports criticizing or endorsing opposition to the government and national policy are considered criminal (Lim, 2019).

There is a shortage of data on internet freedom status in the country. Laos has experienced slower internet development than the rest of the region. Recent years have seen significant progress, leading to a substantial increase in the online population – from 2.6 percent in 2002 to 62 percent in 2023, with over 60 percent of adults aged eighteen and above active on social media. From early on, Laotian authorities implemented strict regulations, which was evident in the punishment of online journalists with dissenting views in the early 2000s (Lim, 2019). The repressive internet regime persisted as the online population expanded. In 2014, a repressive internet law criminalized vaguely defined content, "false and misleading information," against the ruling party, and any content undermining "the peace, independence, sovereignty, unity, and prosperity of Lao PDR" (Palatino, 2014). Prohibiting anonymity on social media, the law excessively regulates online space, discouraging citizens from expressing their opinions. In 2019, in a move claimed to curb the spread of fake news, the government mandated registrations for disseminating news on social media, threatening fines and prison sentences for noncompliance.

Notably, in September 2019, Houayheuang "Muay" Xayabouly received a five-year sentence for criticizing the government on social media, highlighting negligence in handling floods in Southern Laos. Despite international calls for her release, Muay remains imprisoned under unfair conditions. In April 2023, activist Anousa "Jack" Luangsuphom, a key administrator of the Facebook page "Power by the Keyboard," survived an attempted murder allegedly by the state's agent. Jack advocated for Lao youth by offering sharp critiques of the one-state party and denouncing the increasing Chinese influence over Laos. These incidents reveal an alarming pattern of attacks on Lao human rights activists who use online platforms to oppose the authoritarian government.

In 2023, the government announced plans to regulate social media usage, warning that individuals within the country using social media to share false news, distort information, or criticize the government could face consequences (Manushya Foundation, 2023). In reality, the government lacks the technical capacity to control social media. Its records, however, suggest that the state frequently utilizes targeted crackdowns and arbitrary arrests to set an example and instill fear among the public. Despite the government's sporadic efforts to censor online criticism, public protests remain rare due to the massive security presence and restrictive laws.

3.5 Malaysia

From Malaysia's independence in 1957 until 2018, the *Barisan Nasional* (BN, National Alliance) coalition held power. Under the BN regime, Malaysia's media landscape operated under strict regulation, with the ruling coalition exerting indirect control through proxy ownership, fostering self-censorship among journalists and media personnel. The government chose not to censor the internet, but practical limitations emerged due to the utilization of media-related and libel laws to suppress dissenting voices online (Lim, 2019).

As of 2023, over 96 percent of the Malaysian population was online, and nearly all adults over eighteen engaged in social media. Digital activism in Malaysia traces two decades to the initial Reformasi wave in 1998–1999. The abrupt dismissal of Deputy Prime Minister Anwar Ibrahim by Prime Minister Mahathir Mohammad in September 1998, accompanied by politically motivated charges, sparked protests that gained momentum online and eventually spilled onto the streets, giving rise to the Reformasi movement. Alternative online information sources like *Malaysiakini* played a pivotal role in expanding public discourse and challenging the government's mainstream media. In the 2000s, despite declining street protests following Anwar Ibrahim's imprisonment, digital activism persisted through the popularity of alternative media outlets and the emergence of blogger activists (Abbott, 2011; Lim, 2016; Pandi, 2014).

This one-decade legacy laid the groundwork for Bersih, an electoral reform movement initiated in 2006. Bersih movement (see Section 4.2.3) successfully organized significant street rallies from 2007 to 2017, contributing to the growing support for oppositional coalitions, the *Pakatan Harapan* (PH, Hope Alliance) and ultimately ending BN's rule in the 2018 election (Khoo, 2020; Johns & Cheong, 2019, 2021; Lim, 2016, 2017b; Tye et al., 2018).

This shift created opportunities for reform and brought about incremental enhancements in civil liberties. However, the landscape is marred by state censorship, orchestrated cyberattacks and disinformation, and ongoing threats posed by criminal prosecutions and investigations linked to social media posts and online expression, persisting as concerns for individuals (Cheong, 2020; Johns & Cheong, 2019). The LGBT+ community reportedly faces persistent online and offline harassment. In June 2021, the government proposed amendments to Sharia law that would penalize social media users for insulting Islam and "promoting the LGBT lifestyle" (Reuters, 2021). Meanwhile, self-censorship is widespread among online journalists and users, particularly when addressing sensitive issues like the official status of Islam, race-related matters, and preferential treatment for Bumiputera – Malays and indigenous people – over Chinese and Indian minorities (Freedom House, 2022).

Furthermore, following the historic 2018 election, the administration of PH collapsed in 2020, leading to a fracturing of the coalition and factionalizing of individual parties (Weiss & Suffian, 2023). The Bersih movement brought expectations for pro-democracy groups aspiring to politics that transcended the dominance of identity politics. The 2022 general election, however, revealed a contrasting story. Thanks partly to Islamist mobilization on social media, notably on TikTok, voters showed substantial support for *Perikatan National* (PN, National Alliance), a coalition that visibly performed race- and religious-based politics (see Section 5.3.1). Despite the "democratic transition" in May 2018 raising hopes for a more civil liberties-friendly political climate, in 2023, those hopes remain unfulfilled (Weiss, 2023).

3.6 Myanmar

Since gaining independence in 1948, Myanmar has continued to undergo unrest and conflict. The coup d'état in 1962 resulted in a military dictatorship. However, following a 2010 general election, the military junta officially dissolved, establishing a nominally civilian government. This transition saw the release of political prisoners, notably Aung San Suu Kyi. Suu Kyi's party, the National League for Democracy (NLD), won the 2012 by-elections and the 2015 general election, resulting in improved foreign relations and eased economic sanctions. In the 2020 general election, NLD secured a clear majority. However, in 2021, the Burmese military orchestrated a coup d'état and has ruled the country since.

Historically, Myanmar has remarkably positioned itself as a pioneer in digital activism within Southeast Asia, even predating the widespread availability of the internet in the country. The genesis of this movement can be traced back to 1995, when Zarni, a Burmese student in the US, established the Free Burma Coalition website. The website became the hub for Burmese activists in exile and the diaspora to connect with others and disseminate materials to support the Burmese people's pursuit of democracy and human rights (Lim, 2019).

In 2004, Myanmar ventured online as the government granted access to a restricted set of government-approved websites known as the Myanmar Wide Web. However, within this controlled digital space, emails with the .mn domain were closely monitored, and access to international websites was limited. Despite these constraints, activists resourcefully fashioned internet cafes and skillfully circumvented government firewalls by utilizing proxy servers to access prohibited sites. This resilience was evident during the 2007 Saffron Revolution, where Burmese bloggers and digital activists played a significant role (Aung & Htut, 2019). They blogged about "the political situation and uploaded videos and footage of eyewitness accounts," globalizing the event (p. 366).

Meanwhile, concerning the Rohingya population, social media, particularly Facebook, has simultaneously heightened racial and religious tensions between the Buddhist majority and the Muslim minority. For several years since 2012, Facebook has functioned as a fertile ground that has fueled the rise of Buddhist ultranationalism against the Rohingyas and intensified polarization within the country (see Section 4.3) (Kyaw, 2020; Passeri, 2019; Rio, 2021).

As of 2023, the entire population had mobile phone access; 44 percent used the internet, and 36.6 percent of adults aged eighteen and above engaged with social media. Despite the postcoup increase in internet access cost, frequent internet shutdowns (Lim, 2020b), and broad restrictions on digital content, social media platforms remain avenues for expressing dissent, as depicted by the 2021 anticoup d'état mass protests (Jordt, Than & Lin, 2021) (see Sections 4.2.1 and 4.4). After the coup, the military had neither gained complete control of the territory nor crushed online dissent, partly due to the vibrancy of the hybrid anti-coup resistance forces, both offline and on social media (Ryan & Tran, 2022).

3.7 The Philippines

After achieving independence in 1946, the Philippines underwent a tumultuous journey that included the overthrow of the decades-long Marcos dictatorship in 1986. Despite often being lauded as the freest nation in Southeast Asia, the country grapples with persistent corruption, cronyism, and nepotism, driven primarily by a select few influential families controlling the economy and politics. Over the past decades, the Philippines has witnessed a decline in freedom. This decline corresponds with political and civil rights erosion under former president Duterte, who concluded his six-year term in June 2022, and the current presidency of Bongbong Marcos Jr., the son of the dictator Ferdinand Marcos Sr.

In 2023, over 73 percent of the population was online, and nearly all adults over eighteen were on social media. In the last two decades, the Philippines has maintained its reputation as the most connected society. Manila was once the capital of texting in the world, then the capital of Facebook. Filipinos are continuously among the most active social media users in the world.

The Philippines has a long-standing history of digital activism. The internet played a crucial role in disseminating information that fueled resistance against President Estrada, leading to his removal from the presidency in 2001. The advent of mobile phones translated online resistance into street protests (Rafael, 2003). In 2013, organized through platforms like Facebook, Twitter, and text messages, hundreds of thousands gathered at Luneta Park in Manila to protest the corruption-tainted development fund (see Section 4.2.2). In the same park, ten years later, on the fifty-first anniversary of the martial law, protesters gathered to oppose the Bongbong Marcos administration.

Social media is a common platform for political discussions, particularly during elections, in the Philippines. Overall, digital activism in the country is vibrant. However, online sources of information have become more susceptible to manipulation by the government and other entities (Ong & Cabañes, 2018). Duterte's presidency and his successor's, Bongbong Marcos', are marked by the prevalence of social media vigilantism, where *cyber-troops*[7] are deployed to distort the online information landscape, aiming to manipulate public discourse (see Sections 5.3.1 and 5.3.2). Meanwhile, threats, arrests, harassment, and attacks on journalists and media figures such as Nobel Laureate Maria Ressa have contributed to a climate where individuals feel deterred from expressing themselves freely online (Freedom House, 2023e).

---

[7] *Cyber-troop* typically describes an individual paid to spread political propaganda online, especially on social media platforms (Lim, 2023a: 188). In Indonesia it is called *buzzer* (see footnote 18) and in the Philippines sometimes called *keyboard warrior.*

3.8 Singapore

Since 1959, Singapore's parliamentary political system has been overwhelmingly influenced by the People's Action Party (PAP) and the legacy of Prime Minister Lee Kuan Yew, the father of the current prime minister, Lee Hsien Loong. While the PAP's established electoral and legal framework allows for a degree of political diversity, it simultaneously curtails the expansion of opposition parties and imposes restrictions on freedoms of expression, assembly, and association (Chua, 2012).

Singapore swiftly embraced the internet, establishing itself as an information services hub. Nevertheless, right from its early stages of development, the government implemented rigorous political control over the utilization and distribution of information among its populace. The Singapore Broadcasting Authority (SBA) takes charge of the internet content regulation scheme, with a specific focus on materials about Singapore's interests, particularly those that have the potential to incite racial or religious hatred (SBA, 2002).

Singapore is a country marked by self-censorship. Nonetheless, the internet offered a more critical space than traditional print media, expanding the public sphere and providing a platform for marginalized individuals to engage with policies (Weiss, 2014: 96). While not highly visible offline, digital activism exists in the country. Its roots can be traced back to 1994 with the emergence of *Sintercom*, an online forum featuring political content and identifying itself as a "civic" organization (Lim, 2019).

Enduring political pressure and stringent censorship, during the 2000s and early 2010s, digital activism in Singapore was expressed through reporting activism and contentious journalism (George, 2006). Platforms like *New Sintercom*, the satirical *Talking Cock site*, the newsgroup portal *The Optical*, the commentary platform the *Void Deck*, and alternative websites such as *Sammyboy* emerged during this period (Lim, 2019). While its actual impact remains uncertain, the surge in support for the Workers' Party and other opposition factions in the 2006 and 2011 general elections, along with the rise of LGBTQ+ rights movements in the country, can be partially credited to social media activism (Lim, 2019; Pang, 2020; Zhang, 2016).

As of 2023, most of the country's population was connected online, with over 89 percent of adults over eighteen actively participating in social media. However, internet freedom in Singapore remains under threat, with the government persistently exerting control over the digital landscape. Recent legislative developments, such as the passage of the 2022 Online Safety (Miscellaneous Amendments) Act and the 2023 Online Criminal Harms Act, exacerbate this trend (Freedom House, 2023f). These new measures, coupled with existing laws like the 2021 Foreign Interference (Countermeasures) Act and the 2019 Protection from Online Falsehoods and Manipulation Act, grant authorities extensive powers to restrict online activities (Pang, 2020).

During 2022–2023, reports emerged of internet users experiencing intimidation, police scrutiny, and criminal charges for sharing political and social content on social media (Freedom House, 2023f). Social media activism persists, but the prevalent atmosphere has led journalists and regular users to exercise self-censorship, driven by anxiety over potential repercussions, leading to self-censorship among journalists and ordinary users.

3.9 Thailand

Apart from short periods of parliamentary democracy in the mid 1970s and 1990, Thailand has episodically alternated between military and civilian governments. The country has experienced numerous regime oscillations due to frequent military coups, totaling nineteen attempts since its transition to a constitutional monarchy in 1932 (Sinpeng, 2021b). *Lèse-majesté* laws, designed to combat defamation against the monarchy, have been widely applied in Thailand, especially following the 2014 military takeover. Despite Thailand's recognition as one of Asia's freest media countries since 1992, nearly 75 percent of *lèse-majesté* charges after 2014 were associated with exercising freedom of expression (FIDH, 2016). The National Council for Peace and Order (NCPO) and the junta-appointed government issued orders prohibiting online content perceived as critical of the monarchy, the NCPO, or the government (Freedom House, 2016). The introduction of a new Computer-Related Crime Act in 2016 granted extensive powers to restrict free speech, enforce surveillance, and retaliate against activists (Freedom House, 2016). The combination of century-old *lèse-majesté* and newer laws has resulted in ongoing suppression of criticism and dissent, notably online.

In 2023, over 93 percent of the population was online, and nearly 85 percent of adults over eighteen were active on social media. Thailand's digital activism has deep historical roots, as seen in early examples from the 1990s, such as the popular newsgroup "soc.cul.thai" (Lim, 2019). Organizations like Thaidemocracy.org leveraged the internet to mobilize volunteers for various causes, and websites like Prachachon.net aimed to provide alternative political information (Lim, 2019). With the widespread adoption of social media in the late 2010s, digital activism has become integrated into street protests by both democratic (Sections 4.2.1 and 4.4) and antidemocratic (Section 4.3) movements (Sinpeng, 2021b). Furthermore, recent times have witnessed digital politics mirroring on-the-ground polarization, where social media at the center of the political contest between the Yellow Shirts

(Section 4.3) – the hyper-nationalist, ultraroyalist, and pro-monarchy – and the Red Shirts – antiestablishment and pro-democracy (Lim, 2023b).

The restrictive control imposed by the military junta has spurred human rights activism online, with coalitions like Thai Lawyers for Human Rights monitoring and documenting violations. Anonymous Facebook pages, such as Stop Fake Thailand, have over half a million followers and provide a platform for individuals to share opinions and organize political activities (Freedom House, 2016). In 2020–2021, social media platforms were heavily incorporated into students' protests against the military junta, making it one of the largest and longest protests in the country's history (Section 4.4).

Social media are central to the Thai elections. The 2019 elections saw the impact of the platforms and first-time voters. The newly established Future Forward Party, with its youthful leader, Thanathorn, and a solid social media presence, specifically the hashtag #Futurista, made a surprising electoral success (Chattharakul, 2019). In 2023, the Move Forward Party (MFP), led by Pita Limjaroenrat, repeated the #Futurista story with a more skillful social media campaign (see Section 5.2.1). The MFP secured a majority but could not govern due to the monarch and the junta's intervention.

3.10 Timor-Leste

Since gaining independence in 2002, Timor-Leste (East-Timor) has effectively navigated internal conflicts and political instability. The country remains relatively impoverished, relying heavily on natural resources and foreign aid to sustain its economy. Despite commendable governmental efforts, substantial challenges persist, particularly in rural areas where 68 percent of the population resides.

Timor-Leste is a relatively young nation with a history of digital activism intricately interwoven with its liberation fight. The internet played a crucial role during the Indonesian occupation; it helped mobilize support and disseminate information within the transnational movement that advocated for the human rights of the East-Timorese and supported East-Timorese pro-independence activists (Simpson, 2004). In 1990, pro-East-Timor activists and human rights groups started "reg.easttimor" newsgroup that allowed information about the East Timor situation, such as the 1991 Santa Cruz massacre, to be disseminated globally (Hill, 2002). Nearing the final years of its struggle for independence, in 1997, the internet domain for East-Timor (.tp) was established. Managed by Connect-Ireland, the domain became the hub for collaborative efforts across diverse international networks (Hill, 2002).

As the telecommunication infrastructure was destroyed during the 1999 political violence, the digital infrastructure only began to be restored in the early 2000s. Though slow and limited, internet connectivity has experienced significant growth, with over 49 percent of the population online in 2023, an exponential increase from just 1 percent in 2009 (Lim, 2019). In contrast, mobile phone access was widespread throughout the entire population, and approximately 40 percent of adults aged eighteen and above were active on social media (Data Reportal, 2023b).

Timor-Leste is regarded as one of the freest countries in Asia. Freedom House (2023a) cited it as Southeast Asia's only "free" country. However, the reality on the ground paints a more complicated picture. With the rapid growth of users, citizens have utilized social media platforms to exercise their free speech, resulting in increased criticism directed at government officials. The government responded by introducing new laws or provisions limiting offline and online expression, such as the 2020 proposal to reinstate a criminal defamation provision to the penal code and the 2021 draft of Cybersecurity Law (Asia Centre, 2021).

Despite its "satisfactory" freedom press status (see Table 3), the government has misused defamation charges to silence its critics. In 2017, Oki Raimundos and Lourenco Martins, two journalists from the *Timor Post*, were charged with defamation for publishing an article about the potential corruption involving Prime Minister Rui Maria de Araujo (IFJ, 2022). The charges, though, were overturned in the same year. Five years later, in 2022, Francisco Simões Belo da Costa, the editor-in-chief of local news portal *Hatutan.com*, was sued for defamation by Francisco Jerónimo, the Minister of Social Communication, over an online report alleging ministerial corruption (IFJ, 2022).

3.11 Vietnam

Vietnam, a long-standing one-party state ruled by the Communist Party of Vietnam (CPV), severely restricts freedom of expression, religious freedom, and civil society activism (Freedom House, 2023g). Despite some technical allowance for independent candidates in legislative elections, most are effectively banned. The CPV not only monopolizes all media levels but also arrests and intimidates those expressing dissenting views (Thayer, 1992).

From the early days of the internet, the state has maintained control over the online sphere. In the late 1990s to the early 2000s, café owners were held responsible for customer messages, leading to the establishment of a national monitoring system to prevent access to politically or morally deemed dangerous websites (RSF, 2003). Vietnam's online environment is one of the most repressive globally, with the government blocking websites deemed politically or morally dangerous, including foreign news sites and those of international civil society organizations. It officially prohibits internet use for political opposition, actions against national sovereignty and security, and violations of morality or the law, often punishing violations with imprisonment.

In 2023, nearly 80 percent of the population had internet access, and almost 90 percent of adults over eighteen were on social media. Authorities have escalated crackdowns on citizens using social media for dissent, pressuring global internet companies for compliance. Since enacting the 2019 Cybersecurity Law, which pressured social media companies to remove compliance, there has been a surge in content removal. Users now share screenshots of articles they expect to be deleted instead of sharing URLs.

Heavy fines are imposed on online publications for disseminating false information. In 2022, the Ho Chi Minh City government fined media outlets 780 million dong ($33,000) for publishing deemed illegal content. Major social media platforms, including Facebook and Google, complied with the government's content restriction requests. Facebook blocked or removed 2,751 posts labeled as false, anti-CPV, anti-state, and defaming in 2022. Google removed 7,935 YouTube videos and geo-blocked seven reactionary channels, with 95 percent of Google's removal requests related to government criticism from July 2022 to December 2022 (Freedom House, 2023g).

Human Rights Watch reports over 160 political prisoners, including bloggers and activists, in Vietnam (HRW, 2024). Despite ongoing detentions and harassment, digital activism persists; the growth of social media users has strengthened digital activism, making the internet a de facto forum for dissenting voices (Section 4.2.1) (Luong, 2020; Vu, 2017).

4 Dynamics of Dissent: Grassroots Activism in the Social Media Age

"Never again, never forget!" The protestors passionately chanted these words while marching toward Rizal (Luneta) Park in Manila to commemorate the anniversary of the declaration of martial law. On September 21, 2023, marking fifty-one years since President Ferdinand Marcos imposed martial law, many demonstrators assembled in the streets and squares of Manila and various locations nationwide. Organized through Facebook and other social media platforms, these protesters expressed collective solidarity, aiming to prevent recurring atrocities associated with martial law. Simultaneously, they voiced opposition to corruption allegations linked to the administration of President Ferdinand "Bongbong" Marcos Jr. and Vice President Sara Duterte.

The September 2023 protest in the Philippines is one among thousands that occurred in Southeast Asia over the past decade. These movements extensively utilized social media platforms, notably Facebook, Twitter, and, more recently, Instagram and TikTok, in various stages – before, during, and after the protests.

Numerous studies from the early 1990s to the present have delved into online politics, generating significant interest in understanding how digital technologies offer avenues for citizen engagement. While certain critics dismiss political participation on social media as mere *slacktivism* or *clicktivism* (Bozarth & Budak, 2017; Morozov, 2011) and attribute it to a lack of substantive meaning, alternative perspectives argue that political engagement should be perceived as a multidimensional concept involving various activities (Koc-Michalska et al., 2014; Seto, 2017). In this context, individuals express opinions, gain insights, form alliances, and exert influence vertically and horizontally. The argument presented here does not advocate prioritizing the digital environment over traditional avenues like the street. Instead, it underscores the emergence of new pathways to engagement and alternative forms of political participation. Moreover, it is evident that, in contemporary activism, the digital and traditional venues (e.g., streets and squares) can no longer be separated (Lim, 2018; Seto, 2017).

Digital platforms, especially social media, offer features that afford the organization of collective action and mass mobilization. *Affordances* are relational concepts defined as "action possibilities and opportunities that emerge from actors engaging with a focal technology" (Faraj & Azad, 2012: 238). The impact of technology, thus, arises not solely from itself or users but from the relationship between users and the material features of the technology. These *affordances* encompass how platforms facilitate user communication and interaction, create opportunities to build relationships across geographical boundaries, and enable easy sharing and distribution of content. Consequently, social media significantly enhances the potential for forming and expanding information networks at a much lower cost than ever.

In this section, the exploration centers on how activists and citizens utilize social media platforms to engage with the power and with each other, focusing on grassroots activism. To address this question, the subsequent texts offer insights from diverse regional cases, presenting empirical and analytical perspectives on the intricate issues surrounding political participation and social media. The discussion begins with an overview of the state of mass protests and grassroots activism in Southeast Asia, followed by sections on progressive and regressive activism and an exploration of the region's binary, affective, and polarized nature of activism.

4.1 Mass Protests in Southeast Asia: An Overview

Despite the prevailing trend toward autocratization (see Section 2.3), grassroots activism and mass protests have thrived in Southeast Asia. This vitality is

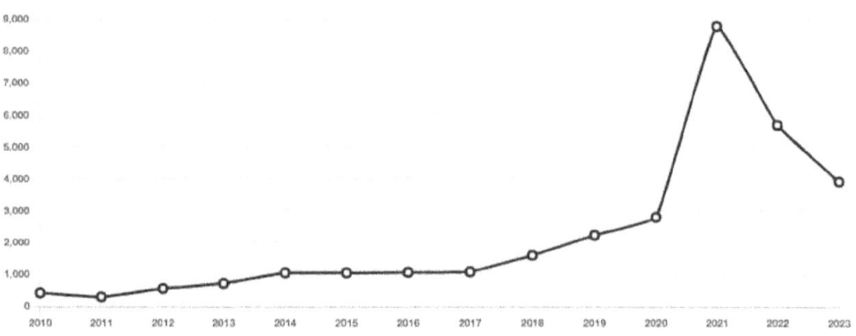

Figure 5 Protests in Southeast Asia (2010–2023)

Source: Author, based on ACLED (2023).

evident in the substantial number of protests recorded throughout 2023, totaling 3,911 from January to November.[8] Noteworthy differentials are apparent in protest frequencies across nations, with Indonesia consistently standing out as the epicenter of such events (see Table 4).[9] In the meantime, the Philippines, known for its historical embrace of protest culture, and Myanmar and Thailand, despite contending with military junta rule, have experienced significant protest activities.

Thousands of protests occurred throughout Southeast Asia in the 2010s and 2020s (Figure 5). In 2021, protests reached a pinnacle, totaling 8,789 occurrences for the year, primarily fueled by extensive and enduring youth-led demonstrations across multiple countries in the region (see Section 4.4). The overarching theme of these 2021 protests was a collective reaction to perceived threats posed by autocratic forces to civil society, and they all incorporated social media into their protest repertoires. The extensive and widespread demonstrations in opposition to the coup d'état in Myanmar in February 2021, which persisted throughout the year, significantly elevated the tally of protest incidents, surpassing 5,000 occurrences in the country alone.

It is impossible to determine the exact number of protests that were organized online. However, given the pervasiveness of mobile social media and people's dependence on mobile phones (see Table 1), it is unlikely for any protest not to have some social media involvement. However, the opposite is not always true. The pattern noted in 2023 (Table 4), along with a more extended trend (2016–2023) (Table 5), underscores that the occurrence of protests in Southeast Asia is not evenly distributed. While the low digital population in Laos and Timor-Leste may

---

[8] Computed from ACLED (2023).

[9] The increase in protests in October–November can be attributed to pro-Palestine rallies that were sparked by the Israeli attacks in Gaza that ensued after the Hamas attack on October 7, 2023.

Table 4 Protest occurrences in Southeast Asia (January–November 2023)[10]

Country	Jan	Feb	Mar	Apr	May	Jun	Jul	Aug	Sep	Oct	Nov
Brunei	0	0	0	0	0	0	0	0	0	0	1
Cambodia	9	11	7	3	8	5	3	5	10	6	6
Indonesia	172	168	274	138	319	222	204	229	217	307	331
Laos	0	0	0	0	0	0	0	0	0	0	0
Malaysia	6	5	9	8	6	5	9	7	7	31	15
Myanmar	92	1	3	60	68	45	73	59	57	50	55
The Philippines	12	26	38	22	29	41	30	22	37	34	57
Singapore	0	0	0	0	0	0	0	0	1	0	0
Thailand	33	11	7	17	20	16	47	18	12	55	21
Timor-Leste	0	1	1	0	0	1	3	0	0	0	0
Vietnam	2	0	0	1	0	0	0	0	0	10	0
TOTAL	326	223	312	249	450	334	369	340	341	492	475

[10] Compiled by author, data from ACLED (2023).

Table 5 Protests in Southeast Asia by country (2016–2023)[11]

	2016	2017	2018	2019	2020	2021	2022	2023
Brunei	0	0	0	0	0	0	0	1
Cambodia	182	95	63	69	96	48	128	75
Indonesia	302	204	768	1,024	1,340	1,620	2,830	2,621
Laos	0	2	1	0	1	1	2	0
Malaysia	N/A	N/A	151	168	48	94	137	109
Myanmar	251	213	233	442	179	5,719	2,011	724
The Philippines	173	391	182	315	302	267	269	358
Singapore	0	0	0	0	2	3	4	1
Thailand	116	157	165	186	820	864	334	299
Timor-Leste	0	0	0	0	4	4	3	6
Vietnam	40	28	37	23	9	0	11	13

[11] Compiled by author, data from ACLED (2023).

tempt us to draw a correlation between technological readiness and the level of activism, such a thesis quickly falls apart when considering other dynamics. Despite its limited technological adoption, Myanmar has experienced a surge in protests.

Meanwhile, notwithstanding a significant social media population, Brunei remains devoid of protests. No inherent technological obstacle prevents social media from playing a role in Brunei. It is the country's sociopolitical dynamics that contributes to the inactivism and absence of protests (see Section 3.1). This reaffirms the earlier assertion that the impact of social media on politics is primarily shaped by the sociopolitical context and user behavior within that specific setting rather than being determined by inherent technological capabilities for collective action.

As discussed in Section 2, Southeast Asia exhibits vibrant social media usage. It is often claimed, sometimes without solid empirical evidence, that social media platforms significantly shape public activism (Jost, Barberá & Bonneau, 2018; Shirky, 2011). However, establishing a correlation between the high usage level and the occurrence of protests is intricate, and identifying the direct causes and consequences of social media use remains immensely challenging (Jost et al., 2018).

In scrutinizing the complex entanglement of communication and media in the making of social movements, my previous research identified that these platforms are very part of movements' *imaginaries*, *practices*, and *trajectories* (Lim, 2018) (Figure 6). Social media platforms, in this context, are part of activists' journey through these modes, and embedded in mechanisms through which "social movements, communicative practices, and actions on the grounds are interconnected and unraveled in space and time, such as *dis/connecting, brokering, bridging, framing, hybridizing (repertoires of contention), in/visibility, intermodality, on/offline connectivity,* and *globalizing*" (Lim, 2018: 103). These mechanisms are part of activists' complex works, such as cultivating shared grievances, expanding networks of resistance, and building resilience against repressions. As such, social media platforms were not the sole cause of the proliferation of protests in Southeast Asia. They were, however, part of activists' repertoires in generating grassroots activism. Furthermore, external factors, such as the prohibition of protests and the use of force in curtailing protestors, also played an important role.

Political protests have a long history, but the capability to access real-time accounts of protest actions and conversations through social media platforms is novel. Locating a protest without its distinctive hashtag on Twitter has become increasingly challenging, with these hashtags linking to

Figure 6 Communications and media of social movements: an analytical framework

Source: Lim, 2018: 104.

protestors' messages, their profiles, and social circles. For the interested public, the visibility of protests provides a mechanism to be connected to the activism of their interest. Organizers of protests find social media invaluable for quickly sharing details about various protest-related information and updates, making it easier to coordinate activism. On the flip side, the use of social media by potential dissidents offers governments opportunities to track and suppress dissents. This dynamic sets the stage for an ongoing and never-ending cat-and-mouse game between dissidents and defenders of established authorities (Jost et al., 2018; Morozov, 2011; Shirky, 2011). Furthermore, not all grassroots politics are progressive; the regressive actors and groups (see Section 4.3), too, can exploit social media *affordances* for mobilization.

4.2 Progressive Grassroots Activism

The years 2010s–2020s have been marked by a multitude of progressive mass protests. These include the Bersih rallies (Section 4.2.3) in Kuala Lumpur (2007, 2011, 2012, 2015, and 2016), the oppositional protests in Phnom Penh (2013–2014) (Section 4.2.1), and more recently, the pro-democracy protest movements in Thailand and Myanmar in 2020 and 2021 (Sections 4.2.1 and 4.4).

It is essential to acknowledge that even before the emergence of social media, the internet had already been involved in significant protest events during the late 1990s and early 2000s. Events such as the *Reformasi* movements in Indonesia (1998) and Malaysia (1998–2000), the "People Power II" protests in the Philippines (2001), and Burma's "Saffron Revolution" (2007–2008) were all predisposed to the presence of the internet.[12] In the following decades, these countries continued to be riffed with grassroots activism, and the incorporation of social media platforms intensified. History matters. Here, the early adoption of digital media in grassroots politics in the late 1990s and early 2000s laid the groundwork for the subsequent integration of social media into future activism. Particularly noteworthy is that the two-decade history of Malaysian online–offline activism from the 1990s played a pivotal role in the relative success of the Bersih electoral reform movement in the 2010s (see Section 4.2.3).

The introduction of social media to Southeast Asia signals a distinct era of digital activism. On the one hand, these platforms offer opportunities for civil society groups and activists to communicate, build networks, distribute content, and organize mass activism. However, the expansive nature of social media networks, the abundance of content, short attention spans, and fragmented conversations pose challenges (Lim, 2013: 644). In this environment, civil society faces the task of countering the trend toward shrinking soundbites (Lim, 2013: 651) and addressing algorithmic biases that favor simplistic and emotionally charged extreme content (Lim, 2020a).

During this period, activism has navigated the landscape of *algorithmic politics*, characterized by *algorithmic enclaves* (Section 1.3) and *affective binary framework* (Section 4.2.2) that can both facilitate and hinder civic and democratic pursuits. Moreover, the social media landscape in Southeast Asia, in contrast to the early days of the internet, is intertwined with increased state control and surveillance, operating within an autocratizing trend (see Section 2.3).

4.2.1 Rights Activism in Authoritarian Settings

Despite facing a repressive environment, grassroots activism persists in authoritarian countries such as Cambodia, Myanmar, and Vietnam. In these countries, activists and citizens continue to express dissent despite their governments' relentless suppression of free speech. High-profile social media activists face arrests and persecution, yet the spirit of resistance endures.

---

[12] See Lim 2023b: 26–35 for activism in the static internet era from the 1990s and mid 2000s and blogging activism from the mid 2000s to the early 2010s.

In Cambodia, activists utilize social media to document and record human rights violations, especially concerning land grabs. An early exemplary case is Venerable Luon Sovath, a Cambodian Buddhist monk who actively used his mobile phone to document land rights abuses nationwide. In 2009, during a forced eviction in Siem Reap province, Sovath, also known as the "multimedia monk," captured video evidence on his phone, revealing police shooting at helpless villagers (Chak, 2014). In 2020, he was forced to leave Cambodia to escape government persecution and is currently living in exile in Switzerland.

Social media played a crucial role in a series of protests in Phnom Penh, Cambodia, peaking in late December 2013 and January 2014. The demonstrations revolved around contested national election results in 2013 and workers' rights, calling for an elevated minimum wage for garment workers. Supporters of the now-disbanded Cambodian National Rescue Party (CNRP), the primary opposition, united with striking workers and other dissatisfied factions. In Phnom Penh, tens of thousands gathered, advocating for changes in the nation's political, social, and economic spheres. The surge in protests was fueled by increased access to information, mainly through mobile phones and social media. Platforms like Facebook and Twitter played a central role in swiftly disseminating information about the social conflicts driving the protests and the protests themselves. The widespread online sharing of photos and videos depicting state violence against demonstrators further amplified the impact of these events.

Despite the Communist Party's enduring control over the internet in Vietnam, social media activism has flourished (Luong, 2020). Platforms like Facebook have become crucial outlets for dissent against the party's influence (Bui, 2016). They facilitate people to express their opinions, especially on development-related issues like land disputes and environmental concerns. One notable instance is the Trees Movement, a citizen-led movement protesting the Hanoi government's decision to cut down numerous large old trees along the city's streets in 2015. Using social media as a platform for collective resistance and action, the movement empowered people and raised awareness of their citizenship rights, potentially influencing state–society relations in Vietnam (Vu, 2017). Additionally, amid crackdowns and activist arrests, Facebook is a vital tool for monitoring detained activists, organizing visits and vigils, and gathering donations for political prisoners (Wallace, 2017).

Despite severe internet freedom violations and legal restrictions in Myanmar, activists and citizens utilized social media to share information and videos exposing protests, repression, and human rights abuses. Following the coup by the military junta in 2021, civil society groups and independent news outlets employed digital platforms to monitor protests and human rights violations through crowdsourcing and mapping applications. Simultaneously, online petitions and social media campaigns sought international support, pressuring governments and organizations to act against the military regime. A notable case of social media activism arose from the case of Kyal Zin, who was shot by security forces in Mandalay in 2021 while protesting. The phrase on Kyal Zin's t-shirt, "Everything will be ok," went viral, prompting a tribute song on the We Click YouTube Channel, renowned for supporting Myanmar's revolutionary movements. During the 2021 Spring Revolution, hashtag campaigns like #WhatsHappeninginMyanmar were vital in effectively enhancing the global call for attention. Activists in this movement strategically utilized online platforms, particularly Facebook and Instagram, to generate anti-junta posts, which were then translated into offline protests.

4.2.2 Issue-Driven Activism: Corruption and Political Scandals

In the absence of a definitive adversary akin to authoritarian governments, grassroots activism in less-authoritarian environments takes on a different form, diverging from traditional political engagement. Unlike traditional protests rooted predominantly in identity, this activism tends to focus more on specific issues. In this scenario, diverse groups lacking a shared belief system may find common ground by rallying around a shared issue or a mutual adversary.

Issue-driven activism is apparent in the relatively open societies of Indonesia and the Philippines. Corruption, a significant sociopolitical concern, is a central focus of protests in these countries. It is considered one of the region's most widespread political issues, with most political scandals related to corruption. In Southeast Asia, the intricate connection between business and politics gives rise to various manifestations of corruption. Clientelist networks facilitate the exchange of gifts or favors by politicians for political backing, while dynasties and affluent business figures wield influence over political parties (Ufen, 2017). At the same time, public awareness of dubious practices has grown, and citizen activism on social media has broadened the scope to examine politicians' lifestyles and business transactions.

In 2009, a significant and pioneering instance of corruption-related social media activism in the region emerged. Dubbed the "one million Facebookers," many Indonesians mobilized on Facebook to rally behind *Komisi Pemberantasan Korupsi* (KPK, Corruption Eradication Commission). This movement primarily aimed at safeguarding KPK commissioners rather than being solely an anti-corruption initiative. The catalyst for this activism was the threat posed by the Indonesian National Police, particularly *Bareskim* (Criminal Investigation Unit), who attempted to criminalize KPK commissioners. In a case widely known as the

"Gecko vs. Crocodile", social media users rallied to support the gecko, symbolizing the seemingly powerless KPK, against the formidable opponent the crocodile represents, the police (Lim, 2013). This movement gained traction on social media, marking Indonesia's first significant instance of social media activism. It subsequently translated into mass protests nationwide, culminating in a 5,000-person rally in Jakarta. The momentum of this movement experienced a resurgence in 2012 and 2015, markedly with the hashtag #SaveKPK (Suwana, 2020).

Similarly, in 2013, social media platforms such as Facebook, Twitter, and text messages were pivotal in orchestrating the "Million People March" in the Philippines. The protest was fueled by the revelation of the "Pork Barrel Scam," a political scandal that implicated multiple Congress members in misusing their discretionary funds for national development projects (commonly termed "pork barrel") by the Philippine Daily Inquirer. The exposure sparked the creation of the Facebook event "Million people march to Luneta August 26: *Sa araw ng mga Bayani. Protesta ng Bayan*!!" (On [National] Heroes Day. People's Protest!!) by Arnold Pedrigal and Bernardo Bernardo, originating from Ito Rapadas' post condemning the scam.

The protest gained momentum with widespread support on social media, employing hashtags #MillionPeopleMarch and #ScrapPork, effectively mobilizing Filipinos for in-person demonstrations on August 26, 2013. On the eve of the protests, 18,000 people had already gathered at Luneta Park, and on the day itself, an estimated 100,000–150,000 attended the rallies. This movement evolved, featuring major protests nationwide and overseas. Despite the protests' massive visibility, the movement's demands, including abolishing the pork barrel system, accountability for misused funds, and punishment for those responsible, were unmet.

Although both were labeled anti-corruption activism, these endeavors and other corruption-related protests in the region are more accurately framed as grassroots initiatives opposing corrupt elites (Lim, 2023b). As symbolized by the gecko versus the crocodile and "a million people" label, they are cast as a contestation between "we, the people" and "them, the corrupt elites," akin to the David versus Goliath story. At the core of this type of mobilization is the appeal to affect. Hence, we see the ascendancy of an *affective binary framework* where binary narratives and rhetoric are employed to cultivate extreme affect, notably rage, as a method of unifying "we" against "them." After all, politics, in all its forms, revolves around emotions, with various parties, ideologies, and movements mobilizing different emotions and infusing their discourse with specific affective markers (Cossarini & Vallespín, 2019: 5).

In subsequent years, social media activism throughout Southeast Asia has adopted a similar *affective binary framework*. In Malaysia, despite the threat against freedom of speech, press, and expression, notably by the politicization of the 2015 Sedition Act, in 2016, online journalists, bloggers, and social media activists mobilized against Prime Minister Najib Razak over his entanglement in a corruption scandal of the state investment firm 1MDB. Employing hashtags such as #1MDB, #DearNajib, and #NajibletakjwtanPM, the movement successfully appealed to public outrage, strengthening a movement calling for Najib to step down.

In the Philippines and Indonesia, social media mobilization continues to revolve around political scandals that provoke public anger. Various materials related to these scandals proliferate on Pinoy and Indonesian social media platforms, purporting to serve as evidence of entrenched elite corruption, with TikTok videos emerging as the dominant form in the 2020s. These materials range from leaked videos showcasing instances of corruption to TikTok testimonial videos of the purported victims of bribery. In these two countries, while social media campaigns fueled by scandals adeptly bring attention to corruption issues, their efficacy in instigating substantial systemic change remains severely restricted (Lim, 2023b). In Malaysia, Bersih activists incorporated the 1MDB scandal into the electoral reform movement, making it one of the factors influencing public discourse, resulting in the fall of BN, Najib Razak's coalition, in 2018.

The *affordances* of social media facilitate the swift spread of information. Nevertheless, these features do not guarantee equal chances for all content types to attain viral status. Virality continues to be an exception, with most content reaching only a restricted audience. The social media landscape is extensive, flooded with content, and characterized by short attention spans – a phenomenon commonly referred to as the economics of attention (Lanham, 2006) – and the economics of emotion. Therefore, in the context of activism, the potential for a message to go viral does not necessarily align with its democratic significance. Instead, it is closely linked to its meme-ability, referring to how much a piece of content resembles a meme – an easily digestible package of information capable of quickly grabbing users' attention – and its affective appeals (Lim, 2023a).

Consequently, social media activism often results in "many clicks but few sticks," indicating the majority of activism failed to generate mass support or attain virality (Lim, 2013). Activists can leverage social media for various causes, but the landscape favors activism that aligns with branding logic and can be easily adapted into a meme format. In such a context, it becomes more feasible for reductionist narratives, such as inherently binary issues or those strategically mobilized with *affective binary framework*, to penetrate social networks.

4.2.3 Mobilized and Deliberated Citizens: Bersih Movement in Malaysia

Although it has a mobilizing effect, social media platforms are notably inadequate in fostering public deliberation, a critical aspect of democratic civil society and social change. Indeed, a deliberative component is notably lacking from the majority of progressive activism in the region. Furthermore, the rapid mobilization facilitated by social media poses the risk of being "too fast, too thin, and too many" (Lim, 2013). As a result, most activism is also largely temporal and ephemeral. In both counts, Bersih, a longitudinal movement that combined both deliberation and mobilization, is a notable exception.

Named after the word "clean" in Malay, the Bersih movement was founded in 2006 to address concerns about electoral irregularities and lack of transparency in Malaysia (Khoo, 2020). Advocating for clean and fair elections, electoral reforms, and good governance, Bersih gained prominence through large-scale rallies in 2007, 2011, 2012, 2015, and 2016. Activists, opposition politicians, and ordinary citizens proliferated the streets and squares of Kuala Lumpur and other cities, united in their demands for reform.

Since its inception, Bersih has recognized the central role of digital media in propelling its movement. Its digital operations have evolved over the years, with initial emphasis on websites, blogs, YouTube, and occasional usage of Flickr. Blogging, a natural choice during the peak of Malaysian political blogging, was significant in Bersih's early stages. The importance of blogging in the movement is tied to the enduring Malaysian blogosphere since 2002, where, despite most blogs being nonpolitical, top bloggers were often politically engaged. A 2007 survey revealed that nine out of Malaysia's top fifty bloggers were political, with eight expressing criticism toward the ruling coalition, BN (Lim, 2017b).

The symbiotic relationship between activists and the blogosphere created an empowering online civic space, challenging authorities and providing reformists a platform for alternative narratives (Johns & Cheong, 2019; Lim, 2016; Smeltzer, 2008). While blogging facilitates conversations, its limited reach emphasizes the need for diverse tools to advance social movements beyond the blogosphere. Bersih's incorporation of YouTube and Flickr in 2006, along with Facebook in 2008 and Twitter in 2011, strategically followed the tools' popularity among Malaysians, especially the youth (Khoo, 2020; Lim, 2017b).

While Facebook played a crucial role in Bersih's preparations by facilitating discussions on protest sites and gathering locations, and Twitter coordinated the protests and made the resistance visible (Figures 7 and 8), they fell short in enabling in-depth deliberations on complex issues. In later years, as a substitute for blogging,

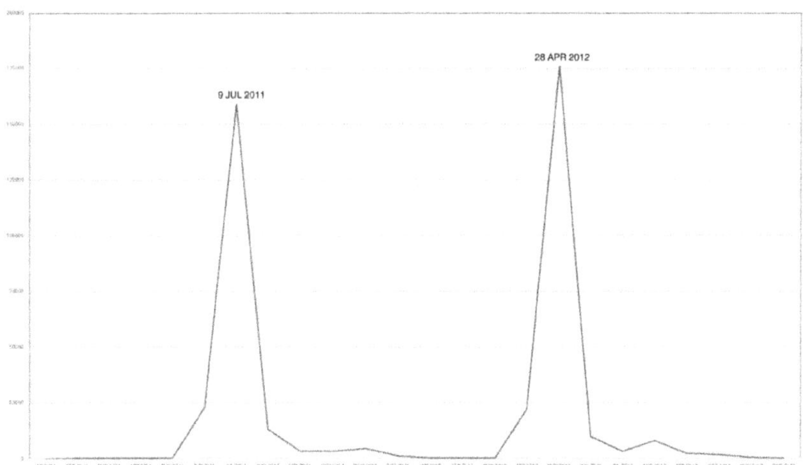

Figure 7 Twitter conversations around Bersih peaked on protest days on July 9, 2011 (Bersih 2.0 rally), and April 28, 2012 (Bersih 3.0 rally)

Source: Author.

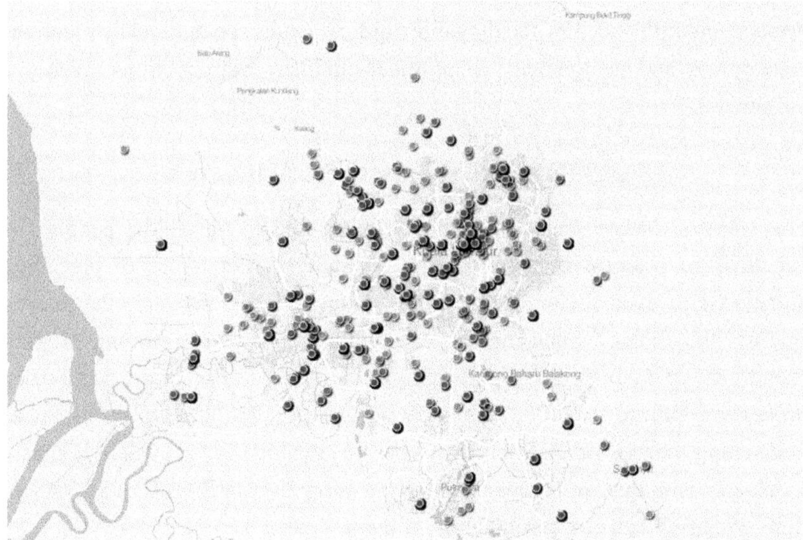

Figure 8 Central Kuala Lumpur map of Bersih tweets, April 28, 2012, 01:00–7:00 pm (GMT+8)

Source: Author.

Bersih utilized WhatsApp (Johns & Cheong, 2021) as a clandestine space for democratic deliberations and small-group discussions alongside face-to-face meetings.

The Bersih movement faced challenges, including government resistance, police crackdowns, and legal restrictions (Johns & Cheong, 2019, 2021; Khoo, 2020; Lim, 2017b). Despite these obstacles, Bersih has raised awareness about electoral issues and advocated for democratic reforms in Malaysia, reflecting a broader desire for transparency, accountability, and democratic governance. In the 2018 election, the movement contributed to the growing support for the opposition, PH, and, subsequently, the end of BN's ruling.

The Bersih case not only demonstrates the potential for cultivating democratic spheres in social media but also emphasizes that transformative civil society activism requires a sustained process integrating mobilization and deliberation across digital and in-person contexts, encompassing both public and private spheres. However, several caveats must be noted. Despite creating horizontal conversational networks, the reliance on social media platforms did not help Bersih eliminate traditional boundaries of party politics or racial dynamics. Also, while some of Bersih's activists may have transcended ethnoreligious divides, these cleavages persist in Malaysian society. Furthermore, in the post-2018 election era, Bersih's capacity to mobilize for change is constrained and influenced by the dynamic political landscape marked by recurrent breakdowns and realignments of political alliances and coalitions (Weiss & Suffian, 2023).

4.3 Regressive Grassroots Activism

The *affective binary framework* can be harnessed to unite "the people" as "victims" in progressive activism against authoritarian forces or perceived injustice. However, it can also be easily manipulated to mobilize the masses against "the Others." Such rhetoric can fuel animosity by exploiting existing resentment or suspicion. By portraying individuals as "victims," the *binary framework* can be exploited to justify actions against "the Others" seen as threatening their space. In Southeast Asia, this exploitation is evident in grassroots activism that embraces hyper/ultranationalist, antidemocratic, radical right-wing politics, or a combination of them.

An illustrative case is Myanmar, where Facebook has served as a fertile ground since 2012 for the right-wing Buddhist ultranationalist movement to exploit *algorithmic politics* and mobilize anti-Muslim sentiment (Kyaw, 2020; Passeri, 2019; Rio, 2021). Although the movement predates the social media era, Facebook has streamlined the mobilization of its anti-Muslim rhetoric, frequently employing extreme speech and disinformation. The algorithmic dynamics of Facebook not only tolerated extreme speech targeting the

Rohingya, such as those disseminated by the *969 Buy-Buddhist* campaign and *Ma Ba Tha* (the Organization for Protection of Race and Religion), but also granted it visibility (Kyaw, 2020). These dynamics promoted the creation of exclusive anti-Rohingya *algorithmic enclaves* and facilitated their expansion. Within these enclaves, particularly on Facebook, hyper/ultranationalist narratives depicting Rohingya Muslims as unpatriotic, a looming threat to the Buddhist majority, and even as terrorists deepened existing divides and anti-Muslim sentiment in Burmese society.

In Thailand, *algorithmic politics* have broadly empowered the Yellow Shirts, the antidemocratic movement centers around the monarchy and military. Studying the 2014 Thai coup, Sinpeng (2021b) posited that social media, particularly Facebook, helped the Yellow Shirts and like-minded ordinary Thais rally support for authoritarianism. The platform played a pivotal role in setting the stage for the coup by facilitating swift and widespread dissemination of antidemocratic sentiments. She contended that social media's ability to amplify such voices, reaching a broad audience at unprecedented speeds, directly contributed to lowering the overall expenses associated with initiating a military coup, and thus significantly streamlined the process of the coup.

In Indonesia, grassroots activism around the 2017 Jakarta gubernatorial race reveals a right-wing Islamist group known as the Muslim Cyber Army (MCA) surfaced around late 2016. The MCA activists used social media to mobilize Muslims by propagating the idea that Islam is under threat. The public emergence of MCA coincided with the 2017 Jakarta gubernatorial election when they lent support to hardline Islamist factions such as *Front Pembela Islam* (FPI, Islamic Defender Front) and actively participated in mobilizing rallies against the then governor Ahok, a Christian-Chinese Indonesian, who made an ill-advised remark about a Quranic verse. Their strategy involved circulating disinformation and incendiary material that was predominantly anti-Christian and anti-Chinese Indonesian, calling Ahok's supporters Chinese infidels, morally corrupt, *haram* (forbidden), and derogatorily referred to them as pigs (Lim, 2017a).

In response, a pro-Ahok *cyber-army*[13] emerged, comprising ardent supporters of Ahok, both voluntary and paid activists. In the name of pluralism and nationalism, the pro-Ahok *cyber-army* engaged in disinformation dissemination and hate speech aimed at branding anti-Ahok individuals as unpatriotic, anti-nationalistic, and traitorous elements. Pejorative terms such as terrorists, *preman berjubah* (robe-clad thugs), *kaum bumi datar* (flat-earth people), *bani koplak* (the idiot tribe), and *kaum onta* (camel people) were

---

[13] The term *cyber-army* is typically used in reference to a group of soldiers highly skilled in information technology with cybersecurity skills. In the case of MCA and Ahok's *cyber-army*, the term is used as a substitute for *cyber-troops* (see note 7).

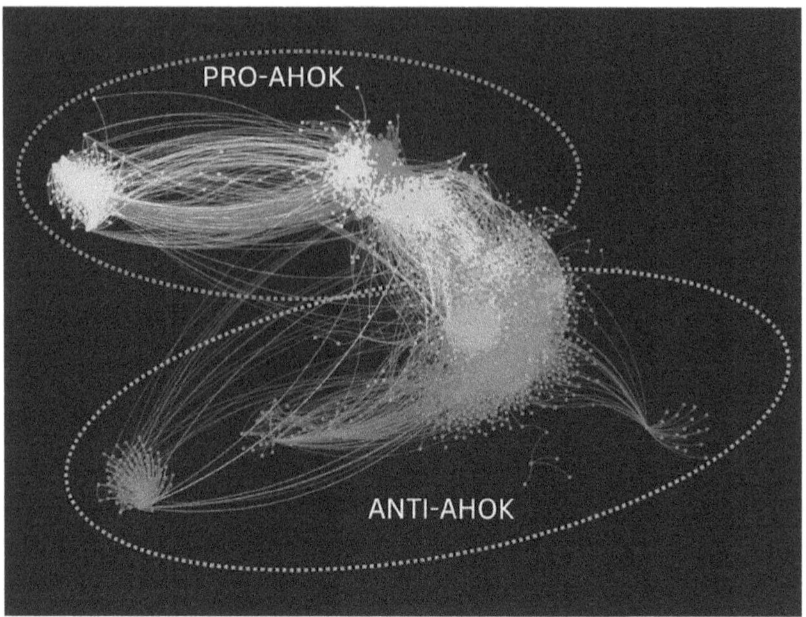

Figure 9 Polarized clusters of anti- and pro-Ahok on Twitter
Source: Author.

used to malign those critical of Ahok (Lim, 2017a). Both factions operated in opposing binaries within exclusive *algorithmic enclaves* primarily unified by perceived threats from "the Others" (Figure 9). The anti-Ahok *cyber-army* bonded over their exclusion of Chinese and non-Muslim Indonesians (mainly Christians), while the pro-Ahok faction excluded Arab Muslims, and some elements displayed Islamophobia.

Meanwhile, in Malaysia, right-wing and ultranationalist groups formed radical and exclusive *algorithmic enclaves* that revolved around the 3Rs: race, religion, and royalty. Historically, the Malay nationalist party UMNO (United Malays National Organization) politicized the 3Rs and portrayed itself as the protector of the interests of ethnic Malays, Islam, and Malaysia's royalty/rulers. The 3R grassroots activism became prevalent after the UMNO's defeat in the 2018 election, which created a "vacuum where Malays need to defend Malays" (Asia Centre, 2023). These 3R defenders engage in harmful tactics, such as online patrolling, doxing, and using hate speech, to attack those who criticize the 3R discourse. For example, not only did they campaign against LGBT people but they also surveilled LGBT activists online and offline. They also filed reports against those they disagreed with to law enforcement and internet service providers and even incited violence (Asia Centre, 2023).

The examples reveal how emerging exclusionary *algorithmic enclaves* can produce multiple forms of tribal nationalism. These enclaves, under the guise of their own brand of nationalism, resort to exercising "freedom to hate" to limit the freedom of "the Others" (Lim, 2017a). Whether Buddhist ultranationalists, Thai ultraroyalists, Indonesian right-wing Islamist factions along with their ultranationalist adversaries, or Malaysian right-wing ultranationalists, they all construct their nationalism on tribalism rooted in shared identity politics that unite people through an exclusionary transcendental solidarity that asserts privileges for its members while negating the rights of "the Others."

Furthermore, all these instances illustrate the mobilizing effect of social media and the effectiveness of the *affective binary framework* in grassroots activism. Here, it is crucial to differentiate between mobilizing and democratizing. Mobilizing is a mechanical process that can align with democratic, autocratic, or other values. My intention is not to undermine the progressive nature of the already-mentioned cases in Section 4.2. Instead, my intervention seeks to critically examine successful social media activism, focusing specifically on the processes and mechanisms leading to their widespread circulation and popularity rather than assessing the values promoted by the activism.

While social media platforms have facilitated mobilization, they were not designed initially to nurture democratic discourse or cater to civic practices. As already discussed, these platforms are deeply entrenched in *algorithmic marketing culture*. Consequently, the mobilizing effect for collective action is simultaneously an outcome of activists' efforts and issue salience and a by-product or unintended consequence of the algorithmic and marketing-driven pursuit of virality.

4.4 Transregional Youth Activism: Hope for the New Politics?

In the context of diminishing room for civic activism and the dominance of authoritarian practices across Southeast Asia, it is vital to recognize the impactful wave of youth activism that has swept through the region in the past four years.

In September 2019, Indonesia experienced its most significant youth protest in two decades, known as #ReformasiDikorupsi (the reform was corrupted), aiming to repeal the Criminal Code Revision Bill and legislation curbing the KPK's authority. Leveraging social media, #ReformasiDikorupsi involved a diverse coalition of campus and noncampus groups, cultivating democratic values and empowering political agency (Sastramidjaja, 2020). The protest strategically utilized hashtags on cardboard signs, blending activism on social media and in the streets, showcasing a keen awareness of digital connectivity as a defining aspect of their movement.

Several months later, in 2020, a second wave of youth protests emerged against the Omnibus Law for Job Creation, a stringent law aimed at streamlining labor and investment legislation. Due to the COVID-19 pandemic, the protest predominantly shifted online, using hashtags such as #TolakOmnibusLaw (reject Omnibus law) and #MosiTidakPercaya (vote of no confidence), trending on Twitter (Sastramidjaja & Rasidi, 2021). By September, messages opposing the Omnibus Law dominated the online sphere. However, by mid October, the government's pro-Omnibus Law messages had gained traction online (Sastramidjaja & Rasidi, 2021) (Section 5.3.2). By the year's end, these protests waned. Nevertheless, remnants persisted in occasional smaller protests and grassroots activism across social media platforms, where the budding collective resistance continued to thrive.

In the same year, amidst the Thai military rule, young activists harnessed the power of Twitter to share information and construct a collective narrative of resistance. The hashtag #FreeYouth was employed during the initial phases of the 2020 anti-government protests (Sinpeng, 2021a). Beyond this phase, activists continued utilizing Twitter to mobilize pro-democracy protests, resulting in more than 1,516 street protests throughout Thailand in 2021. Through hashtags such as #28FebMob, #18JulMob, and #7AugMob, Twitter served as a tool for disseminating information, expressing grievances, providing moral support, mobilizing participants, and issuing calls for action (Charoenthansakul & Natee, 2023).

The resilience of the 2020–2021 Thai protest movements stems from innovative strategies of the youth, particularly on social media and through cultural creativity. Amid rising COVID-19 cases, Thai protesters, including high schoolers, connected with the #MilkTeaAlliance in Hong Kong and Taiwan, embraced online solidarity, and shifted to virtual organizing employing Facebook, Twitter, Instagram, and TikTok. A decentralized network structure enabled swift mobilization, reminiscent of Hong Kong's flash mobs and guerilla "be water" tactics (Teeratanabodee & Wasserstrom, 2024). Protesters cleverly embraced pop culture, dressing as "Harry Potter" characters to subtly criticize the monarchy and military junta. They adopted a meme-worthy three-finger salute from the "Hunger Games," the gesture that first became a pro-democracy symbol in the aftermath of the 2014 Thai coup d'état. The salute was initially seen as humor but eventually became a symbol to convey anti-authoritarian sentiments and highlight a collective awareness of restricted speech in a declining democracy.

Originating in 2020 as an anti-China meme, #MilkTeaAlliance has evolved into a platform for online youth resistance across Asia. In Southeast Asia, it connected various nodes of resistance against perceived authoritarian forces in Indonesia, Thailand, the Philippines, Malaysia, and Myanmar. Particularly prominent during Myanmar's post-coup uprising in 2021, the #MilkTeaAlliance facilitated information dissemination, organized pop-up rallies, and coordinated resistance efforts. Despite a violent crackdown by the junta, activist youth remained resilient, utilizing digital tools for communication, fundraising, and envisioning a democratic post-junta future. The alliance fostered inclusive discussions on citizenship rights and social justice, involving Burmese overseas students and exiles, contributing to a collective effort for positive change (Jordt et al., 2021).

The #MilkTeaAlliance demonstrates Southeast Asian activists' desire for a durable transregional solidarity network and platform to exchange experiences, information, and resources. Sastramidjaja (2024) proposes that the network resembles a *rhizome* (Deleuze & Guattari, 1987), as they are characterized by connectivity, heterogeneity, multiplicity, and expandability. The rhizomatic nature of the #MilkTeaAlliance allows for fluid participation of diverse parties, including nonactivist groups such as K-pop fans, and the incorporation of various injustice-related issues and demands, and increased viability and resilience to repression (Sastramidjaja, 2024).

In the face of government repression, youth activism in the region exemplifies the dynamic, imaginative, and transnationally connected citizenry of Southeast Asia's emerging political generation. The progressive faction of the "digital generation" plays a crucial role in shaping the political discourse and potentially influencing the future trajectory of politics in the region. While their physical presence may have diminished on the streets, their transnational and interconnected networks persist. This rhizomatic movement displays the limit of *communicative capitalist* logic and *algorithmic marketing culture,* as the progressive youth transformed social media platforms into the spheres for alternative and radical imagination that radically depart from the dominant imaginaries of the state (and other sources of hegemony) (Lim, 2018: 106). Within these spheres, the youth nurture a radical vision for the region's future that envisions a more democratic, just, and humane Southeast Asia. This imaginative outlook is a foundation for fostering solidarity and continuing the struggle against oppression.

4.5 Mobilizing but Not Always Democratizing: A Summary

This section explores the complex interplay between social media, activism, and democracy in Southeast Asia, highlighting the potential for positive change and the challenges activists must navigate. On the one hand, social media platforms are instrumental in fostering activism against authoritarian regimes, providing a space for citizens to mobilize against "corrupt elites" and address perceived injustices. Cultivating an *affective binary framework* through social media contributes to solidarity among citizens who share grievances against oppressive regimes.

Conversely, the evolving landscape of social media, marked by algorithmic biases, presents challenges for civil society activism. The algorithmic biases tend to favor extreme and controversial content, making it challenging for moderate voices and civil discourse to gain prominence. The prevalence of an *affective binary framework*, facilitated by *algorithmic marketing culture* on social media, can lead to the polarization of opinions and the exclusion of nuanced perspectives. This framework, driven by the economics of attention and emotion, raises concerns about the potential for social media to be employed for regressive activism that disregards the rights of others.

The Bersih movement stands out among exceptional cases within this challenging algorithmic landscape. It skillfully incorporated deliberation efforts into its activism, utilizing social media to address collective action problems and sustain its efforts over time. By fostering public deliberation, Bersih activists prioritized long-term political reform and societal change over fleeting issues. Nevertheless, even in this exemplary scenario, the limitations of robust social media-driven activism in achieving democracy become apparent.

While it is crucial not to idealize the youth as an unequivocal source of hope and avoid treating them as monolithic, it is essential to acknowledge that the transregional engagement of youth activists in Southeast Asia introduces a hopeful dimension to the discourse. It highlights the potential for a new type of politics that challenges traditional power structures.

Amidst the vibrant landscape of Southeast Asian grassroots activism, challenges such as algorithmic biases, fleeting issues, and potential state interference underscore the need for a nuanced and sustained approach to achieve lasting democratic change. Additionally, as explored in the next section, the state and influential groups, including populist leaders and authoritarian regimes, may harness social media to counter progressive citizen activism, shape narratives, and manipulate public opinion in their favor.

5 Bytes and Ballots: Social Media in/for Political Campaigns and Elections

Throughout history, political leaders have employed diverse communication methods to uphold authority. Roman emperors used coins for widespread propaganda, while modern authoritarian leaders controlled mass media to strengthen their power. Hence, contemporary leaders' strategic use of social media platforms for public communication is a natural evolution of this trend. The late 2000s witnessed the initiation of this practice, and by the close of 2014, over 76 percent of global leaders maintained an active presence on Twitter or Facebook (Barberá & Zeitzoff, 2018).

Before the widespread adoption of the internet, whether it was tactical communication between elites or mass communication reaching the public, traditional communication models generally portrayed the masses as passive recipients of elite messages (Scheufele, 2000). However, the emergence of social media has introduced a new communication paradigm, enabling leaders, whether in positions of power or opposition, to interact with the masses directly, and vice versa. This circumvents traditional media gatekeeping, allowing leaders to reach the public directly and communicate with their support base and adversaries without intermediaries (Zeitzoff, 2017).

As of December 2023, nearly all national leaders in Southeast Asia maintain a presence on social media, focusing on platforms like Facebook and Twitter (X) (see Table 6). Leading the way, Prime Minister Lee Hsien Loong of Singapore was an early adopter, establishing his Twitter account in April 2009. Notably, the most prominent leader on social media is President Joko Widodo (Jokowi) of Indonesia, amassing over twenty million followers on Twitter and ten million on Facebook – understandably, Indonesia is the most populated nation in the region.

After Jokowi, Bongbong Marcos has 7.4 million and 1.3 million followers on Facebook and Twitter, respectively. Cambodia's new Prime Minister, Hun Manet, is notable for his Facebook popularity, with 2.7 million followers, a significant number given the country's population is less than seventeen million. However, this count is considerably lower than his father, former prime minister Hun Sen, who has over fourteen million followers. In 2023, Hun Sen and Jokowi ranked third and fourth among the most followed world leaders on Facebook, following Narendra Modi of India and Joe Biden of the United States. Jokowi also secured positions in the top ten most followed world leaders on Twitter (sixth), Instagram (second), and YouTube (third). President Bongbong Marcos of the Philippines (fourth) and Prime Minister Anwar Ibrahim of Malaysia (ninth) have become some of TikTok's most followed world leaders. In the "like economy," national leaders, too, see the importance of numbers of followers and likes. Here, it is important to note that it is possible to purchase fake likes and followers from "click farmers" or "follower factories," individuals or groups who are readily hired to generate internet traffic in bulk for various purposes.[14]

Leaders may utilize social media for traditional purposes, such as communicating government agendas, showcasing legislative proposals, and influencing public opinion. While traditional goals remain, social media introduces innovative strategies. Leaders can provide insights into their personal lives, offering

---

[14] For more information about click farming, see Lindquist, 2018.

Table 6 Twitter and Facebook accounts of national leaders (by December 2023)[15]

Country	Names	Twitter account	Twitter followers	Twitter following	Joined Twitter	Facebook account	Facebook followers
Brunei	Hassanal Bolkiah	@HassanalBolkia2	2,067	16	February 2014	https://www.facebook.com/profile.php?id=100044322075033	78 K
Cambodia	Samdech Thipadei Hun Manet	@Dr_Hunmanet_PM	48,779	3	August 2022	https://www.facebook.com/Dr.Hunmanetofcambodia	2.7 M
Indonesia	Joko Widodo	@jokowi	20,261,117	58	September 2011	https://www.facebook.com/jokowi	10 M
Laos	Sonexay Siphandone	@sonexay_s	7	1	July 2010	https://www.facebook.com/sonexaysiphandone.29112/	363
Malaysia	Muhyiddin Yassin	@MuhyiddinYassin	1,278,070	17	March 2011	https://www.facebook.com/ts.muhyiddin	2.1 M
Myanmar	Myanmar President Office					https://www.facebook.com/myanmarpresidentoffice.gov.mm	1.8 M
The Philippines	Bongbong Marcos	@bongbongmarcos	1,306,163	37	May 2009	https://www.facebook.com/BongbongMarcos	7.4 M
Singapore	Lee Hsien Loong	@leehsienloong	885,550	27	April 2009	https://www.facebook.com/leehsienloong	1.7 M
Thailand	Srettha Thavisin	@Thavisin	363,303	706	July 2009	https://www.facebook.com/Thavisin.Official	175 K
Timor-Leste	José Ramos-Horta	@JoseRamosHorta1	1,749	129	October 2018	https://www.facebook.com/officialramoshorta	198 K

[15] Compiled by author from Facebook and Twitter by December 2023.

glimpses of leisure time with family, usually through their accounts. Meanwhile, social media can also serve as a tool for international outreach, promoting tourism, and enhancing a country's global image, typically conveyed through the official social media accounts of institutions such as the president's or prime minister's offices.

As illustrated in Table 7, the Facebook pages of Joko Widodo, Hun Sen, and Mahathir Mohamad exhibit substantial interactions with citizens, generating thousands of likes, comments, and shares, surpassing those of institutional accounts. However, predictably, leaders seldom engage directly with citizens on social media, indicating a predominantly one-way and top-down approach. A minimal proportion of leaders' tweets are responses, and they follow a limited number of users (see Table 6), suggesting infrequent exposure to ordinary citizens' tweets.

Beyond these country leaders, politicians of all levels – national and local – and political parties in Southeast Asia have increasingly integrated social media platforms into their political communication strategies, significantly impacting electoral politics in the past decade. This section delves into an empirical and analytical exploration of how politicians and political parties utilize social media platforms for marketing and campaigning, particularly in electoral polit-ics. It highlights their role in shaping voter engagement, disseminating infor-mation, and influencing and even manipulating public discourse. Furthermore, the section discusses how these platforms extend as tools for political propa-ganda and mobilization on various issues beyond the elections, raising concerns about disinformation and deepening polarization.

5.1 Elections in Southeast Asia

Elections are key events in Southeast Asia, not only in more democratic states such as Indonesia and the Philippines but also in authoritarian states. Virtually all countries except Brunei, including one-party states such as Vietnam and Laos, have held elections. In democracies, elections primarily function as a means for citizens to exercise their right to choose their representatives freely and fairly, facilitating the expression of consent. Conversely, in authoritarian regimes, elections fall short of illustrating this principle due to manipulation and misconduct, depriving citizens of a genuine choice (Morgenbesser, 2016). Within authoritarian states, flawed elections are not mere superficial gestures or incremental steps toward democracy; instead, they play a crucial role in sustaining authoritarian rule.

Morgenbesser (2016) argues that authoritarian regimes, such as Singapore, Cambodia, and Vietnam, exploit elections for four essential functions. First,

Table 7 Interactions on Facebook pages of national leaders (by December 2019)[16]

Country	Page section	Facebook	Page	Total interactions	Likes	Comments	Shares
Brunei	Government	facebook.com/bnpmo	Prime Minister's Office of Brunei Darussalam	91	64	11	15
Brunei	Government	facebook.com/govbrunei	GOVBN	13,027	5,588	276	6,820
Cambodia	Prime Minister Hun Sen	facebook.com/hunsencambodia	Samdech Hun Sen, Cambodian Prime Minister	20,489,727	14,243,012	1,127,741	3,394,476
Timor-Leste	Presidency	facebook.com/ EisPresidentiRDTL	Eis Presidente da Republica de Timor-Leste	30,724	25,800	2,474	1,491
Indonesia	President Joko Widodo	facebook.com/Jokowi	Presiden Joko Widodo	39,168,579	29,964,501	2,874,602	2,664,610
Indonesia	Presidency	facebook.com/ KantorStafPresidenRI	Kantor Staf Presiden Republik Indonesia	98,159	72,505	3,100	14,863
Malaysia	Prime Minister	facebook.com/TunDrMahathir	Dr. Mahathir bin Mohamad	9,470,145	5,358,681	1,473,491	1,432,152
Malaysia	Government	facebook.com/PMOMalaysia	PMO Malaysia	13,154	8,846	509	3,132

[16] Compiled by author, data from Twiplomacy (2020).

Myanmar	President U Htin Kyaw	facebook.com/U-Htin-Kyaw	U Htin Kyaw	38,185	28,078	1,281	6,531
Myanmar	Presidency	facebook.com/ myanmarpresidentoffice .gov.mm	Myanmar President Office	1,578,561	1,111,072	30,364	363,461
The Philippines	President Rody Duterte	facebook.com/rodyduterte	Rody Duterte	337,001	268,554	14,242	23,019
Philippines	Presidency	facebook.com/pcoogov	Presidential Communications (Government of the Philippines)	4,115,309	2,135,736	593,210	797,038
Singapore	President Halimah Yacob	facebook.com/halimahyacob	Halimah Yacob	110,807	85,904	6,204	9,704
Singapore	Prime Minister Lee Hsien Loong	facebook.com/leehsienloong	Lee Hsien Loong	1,404,265	1,098,115	78,934	131,449
Singapore	Government	https://facebook.com/gov.sg	Gov.sg	199,208	127,431	9,166	45,936
Thailand	Government	https://facebook.com/ ThaigovSpokesman	ไทยคู่ฟ้า	735,051	404,939	95,648	184,692
Thailand	Government	https://facebook.com/ thailandprd	PR Thai Government	37,314	20,546	1,337	10,671
Vietnam	Foreign Minister Phạm Bình Minh	https://facebook.com/Ph%E1% BA%A1m-B%C3%ACnh- Minh–919861878132744	Phạm Bình Minh	88	67	11	8

elections provide crucial *information*, offering dictators insight into the level of support for the ruling party or opposition in an environment of power insecurity. Second, there is the *legitimation* function, wherein authoritarian rulers use elections to legitimize their authority, seeking moral grounds with normative approval from citizens. This *legitimation* function transforms elections into a theatrical performance, creating the illusion that the ruling party adheres to democratic norms. Third, the *management* function involves keeping political elites in check through tactics such as clientelism, co-optation, solidarity, or succession. Lastly, the *neopatrimonialism* function views elections as a mechanism for distributing patronage to citizens in exchange for their votes to support the ruling party.

In more open states such as Indonesia and the Philippines, elections serve as a platform for citizens to exercise their voting rights with a certain degree of freedom. However, this does not imply that these elections are immune to exploitation. Although the extent of exploitation may be less pronounced, the four functions – information, legitimation, management, and neopatrimonialism – can still influence the electoral process.[17]

Despite the frequent elections in the region, a consistent pattern emerges, characterized by either authoritarian governance or a binary political framework. This framework typically limits opposition or choices, creating an illusion of variety that often conceals the underlying reality. Consequently, voters frequently find their options narrowed down to supporting a specific candidate or opposing that candidate, and this cycle tends to repeat with variations. How social media platforms are utilized for political campaigns, particularly voter mobilization during elections, thus embody this binary structure.

5.2 Social Media Campaigns and Voter Mobilization

Mobilization is key to electoral politics. First, political parties and candidates seek to mobilize supporters through election campaigns and get-out-to-vote initiatives. Research indicates the effectiveness of these efforts in persuading voters to turn out and cast their votes (Gerber & Green, 2000). Second, interpersonal mobilization occurs when members of social networks encourage turnout. In election campaigns, social media functions as a cascading message environment, allowing politicians to tap into interpersonal social networks. This potential for a cascade effect has led elected officials and politicians to increasingly use social media for mobilization, capitalizing on its *affordances* to tap into the extended social networks of supporters. Social media platforms emerge as more potent tools than traditional communication methods, facilitating

---

[17] For a broader and deeper analysis of the elections in Southeast Asia, see Aspinall et al. (2022).

candidate appeals for money, volunteers, and votes through trusted sources – friends and friends of friends within social networks.

The possible linkage between political campaigns and citizen grassroots activism implies the potential for grassroots movements to coalesce around a particular candidate. In such instances, the extensive reach of social media enables candidates to mobilize through cascading effects within volunteer networks and grassroots fundraising. This interplay indicates that nontraditional or perceived outsider candidates now stand a better chance of garnering popularity than historical trends, offering oppositional candidates a competitive advantage. Subsequent discussions explore social media integration into oppositional and outsiders' campaigns in Malaysia, Singapore, Indonesia, Cambodia, and Thailand from the late 2000s to the early 2020s to provide illustrative examples. Illustrations include Jokowi's campaign in Indonesia from 2012 to 2019 and the recent "Pita's fever" case in Thailand in 2023.

5.2.1 The Oppositional and the Outsider Turn

In Malaysia, the integration of digital media began in the 1999 general elections, but it was not until GE13 in 2008 that the platform became a central component of campaigns. In the years leading up to the elections, grassroots activism, notably the Bersih movement (see Section 4.2.3), leveraged social media to bring attention to various sociopolitical issues, including the deteriorating economic climate, corruption, money politics, and the ruling coalition's failure to address the concerns of ethnic minorities. The opposition coalition, along with and supported by Bersih, utilized social media for widespread political mobilization in urban areas. Bersih also employed *intermodality*, linkages between digital and other networks, to mobilize rural voters through mobile phones/SMS and in-person networks (Lim, 2018). The results of the 2008 election were nothing short of phenomenal for the opposition. Although the ruling coalition secured a simple majority, its proportion of the popular vote, parliamentary seats, and state legislatures significantly declined.

In the neighboring country, by 2007, the Singaporean PAP government eased its control over public political discussions, permitting opposition parties to utilize platforms like Facebook, podcasts, and Twitter for campaigning. In the lead-up to the 2011 general elections, opposition parties strategically incorporated social media campaigns, resulting in a significant impact (Pang, 2020). The opposition secured six elected seats, the highest number since independence, including the Workers' Party capturing the Aljunied Group Representative Constituency with five members. The ruling party experienced a decline in the popular vote from 66.6 percent to 60.1 percent, marking its lowest since

1968 (Ortmann, 2016). Various factors contributed to this shift, including social media's role in informing Singaporeans about the opposition, their manifestos, and campaign activities. Social media facilitated the transition of electoral focus from character attacks on the opposition, typically orchestrated by state-sponsored mainstream media in previous elections, to national issues. The platforms provided a cost-effective option for cash-strapped opposition parties to reach a broader audience, allowing Singaporeans to witness substantial turnout at opposition election rallies from the comfort of their homes for the first time (Ortmann, 2016; Pang, 2020).

Meanwhile, in Indonesia, Jokowi's ascent in the 2012 Jakarta gubernatorial election and the 2014 presidential election was intricately tied to an extensive use of social media campaigns. As "outsiders" to Jakarta politics in 2012, Jokowi and Basuki Tjahaja Purnama (Ahok) diverged from their counterparts who heavily invested in television and print advertisements and opted for a firm reliance on social media instead. Their campaigns embraced the marketization and professionalization of social media campaigning, supported by dedicated online and offline voluntary campaigners called JASMEV (Jokowi Ahok Social Media Volunteers). Jokowi's Twitter account, initially created in September 2011 for the gubernatorial election, has since transformed into his official Twitter account and has been consistently utilized in subsequent elections. The Jakarta election set a crucial precedent for social media campaigns in his later electoral pursuits, along with the transformation of JASMEV from a voluntary-based group into a campaign network that included paid *buzzers*.[18]

In Cambodia around 2012–2013, the newly formed Cambodian National Rescue Party (CNRP), led by exiled Sam Rainsy, defied expectations by reducing the ruling CPP's influence in parliament. Limited access to mainstream media led the CNRP to leverage online platforms, including blogs and social media, as a crucial campaign tool. While the CPP controlled traditional media outlets, the CNRP utilized social media to amplify critical voices, addressing grievances against Prime Minister Hun Sen. Online platforms facilitated the dissemination of content, including audio and video clips, exposing unfulfilled promises, gaining significant traction on Facebook (Vong & Sinpeng, 2020), involving the participation of Cambodian civil society organizations and human rights activists in the social media campaign.

In the unfolding historical narrative, the four cases yielded divergent results. In Malaysia, carried by Bersih activists' efforts and Mahathir Mohamad's

---

[18] *Buzzer* is an Indonesian term to describe "a netizen who is paid by a company to disseminate promotional information of a certain product or brand on social media sites" (Lim, 2017a: 417). The political *buzzer* is synonymous with *cyber-troop* (see footnote 7).

leadership, the opposition triumphed in GE14, ending BN's sixty-year rule in 2018. Despite the 2011 setback, Singapore's ruling party, PAP, showcased resilience with a decisive 2015 victory. It did so by partly addressing 2011 election grievances, for example, by initiating citizen feedback and engagement programs and emphasizing constructive political mode over confrontational democracy (Rodan, 2018). Meanwhile, in Indonesia, the Jakarta election's victory set a critical precedent for Jokowi's subsequent social media campaigns, contributing to his victories in the 2014 and 2019 presidential elections. In Cambodia's 2013 election, the opposition CNRP secured fifty-five seats against the CPP's sixty-eight, despite accusations of vote-rigging (Hutt, 2016). Subsequent efforts for reelection proved unsuccessful, leading to a 2014 compromise as the CNRP joined the CPP in parliament. Tensions persisted until 2017 when CNRP leader Khem Sokha faced accusations of treason, and the Supreme Court dissolved the CNRP, imposing a five-year ban on its members' political activities ahead of the 2018 elections.

The narrative of Cambodia's CNRP finds parallels in Thailand's 2023 elections. In this election, a progressive center-left party opposing the military junta, the Move Forward Party (MFP) or *Pak Kao Klai*, succeeded by winning the majority of seats. The party's effective social media campaign was crucial in engaging and mobilizing younger voters. Pita Limjaroenrat, the MFP charismatic leader, surpassed other figures, including the incumbent Prime Minister Prayut Chan-o-cha, in popularity. With over 2.6 million Instagram followers, Pita shared relatable family photos resonating with ordinary Thais. The MFP strategically campaigned on platforms like Facebook, Twitter, Instagram, and TikTok, blending a clear message advocating reform in the monarchy and military with Pita's charismatic persona. This combination led to the phenomenon known as "Pita fever," successfully mobilizing voters, especially the Thai youth. Despite the MFP securing a majority, military-aligned parties and royalist forces utilized all available means to prevent Pita from assuming the role of prime minister.

The divergent outcomes depicted in these cases show that while social media can be pivotal in mobilization and even help the opposition and outsiders leverage their support, it represents just one element within the intricate landscape of politics.

5.2.2 The Authoritarian Capture

Initially, social media campaigns were crucial for oppositional and outsider electoral strategies. However, in the latter years, this approach has seen a rising adoption by authoritarian leaders, ruling parties/coalitions, and status quo proponents.

In Cambodia, in July 2023, social media played an essential role in a controversial election where the main opposition party was barred, and the ruling party, led by long-time Prime Minister Hun Sen, claimed victory, securing almost all seats. Subsequently, Hun Sen's son, Hun Manet, became the new prime minister. After facing rising opposition in the 2013 election, Prime Minister Hun Sen extensively used platforms like Facebook, Twitter, and YouTube to connect with the Cambodian public. His social media efforts intensified leading up to the 2023 election. Anticipating a potential account suspension by Meta, he proactively deleted his Facebook page, which had over fourteen million followers, following the platform's flagging of a video for allegedly inciting violence. After the deletion, Hun Sen encouraged Cambodians to join him on alternative platforms such as Telegram and TikTok. Additionally, he presented a documentary detailing his life on YouTube, signaling a shift in his online presence amid the evolving social media landscape.

Several years prior in the Philippines, Rodrigo Duterte, despite his tie to the Marcos family, orchestrated a successful campaign by successfully positioning himself as a political "outsider" in opposition to the elites. His victory in the 2016 election marked the onset of authoritarian capture. Heavily incorporating social media into his strategies, Duterte's campaign successfully garnered legitimacy from the majority despite its undemocratic practices and antidemocratic ideas. This authoritarian consolidation was solidified in the 2022 election. Duterte's demagoguery style of social media campaigns and Bongbong Marcos' *positive disinformation* (see *algorithmic whitebranding* in Section 5.3.1) helped the son of the long-time dictator Ferdinand Marcos Sr. secure the presidency (Arugay & Baquisal, 2022).

In Indonesia, in 2014, Jokowi initially gained support from progressive and pro-democracy segments, including human rights activists and civil society groups. In the latter part of his first term, however, Indonesian democracy saw a decline due to the manipulation of state institutions for partisan purposes, increased repression of political opposition, and the rise of anti-pluralistic political Islam (Power, 2018). Jokowi further solidified his authoritarian grip ahead of the 2024 election, exemplified by a controversial October ruling from the Constitutional Court allowing his son, Gibran, to run for vice president on Prabowo's ticket. The alliance between Prabowo and Jokowi's social media campaign teams, along with other resources, has given the Prabowo–Gibran duo more leverage than any other candidate and subsequently won the election. The authoritarian turn in Indonesia, ironically, originates from a highly popular (including in social media) and effective president, who was once featured on the cover of *Time Magazine* and portrayed as "a new hope" and "a force of democracy" (Beech, 2014).

5.2.3 Marketing/Branding and Populist Communication Style

Whether oppositional, progressive, or authoritarian, some similarities have run through successful social media campaigns in Southeast Asia. First is that they embrace the principle of political marketing and branding. In the evolving landscape of political campaigns, the influence of commercial frameworks has grown significantly, leading to the integral role of branding in campaign strategy (Scammell, 2007), particularly in social media. In political marketing, "brand" extends beyond its traditional association with commercial products. Instead, it encompasses a political entity's symbolic value and psychological representation, whether a candidate, party, or issue (Scammell, 2007). In this context, a political brand functions as a powerful tool, serving as a "shortcut to consumer choice," enabling the differentiation of entities that may share broad similarities by introducing a layer of emotional connection (Scammell, 2007: 177). The idea here is that voters, much like consumers in a commercial context, are influenced less by the tangible promises and policies put forth by a political entity but more by the brand's affective appeal.

As political campaigns increasingly adopt branding strategies, social media platforms serve as dynamic arenas for cultivating and disseminating political brands. Through visual elements, storytelling, and consistent messaging, campaigns aim to shape and reinforce the symbolic value of their brand. With its vast reach and interactive nature, social media becomes a conduit for establishing and nurturing the emotional connection between the political entity and the electorate. In this way, branding on social media becomes a strategic imperative, especially in electoral politics, influencing how political messages are received, interpreted, and remembered by the voting public. To optimize the chances of content achieving virality, it is crucial for the messaging to align with a robust political branding strategy complemented by a compelling and memorable hashtag, thereby engaging in hashtag politics.

Whether leading up to or during election campaigns and even in nonelection years, politicians actively adopt this political branding approach by integrating social media into their communication strategies, resonating with the prevalent culture of algorithmic marketing. Within this environment, popular politicians, such as Jokowi, Duterte, and Pita, are portrayed as celebrities and idols; they embody the brand.[19]

Furthermore, irrespective of political leanings – centrist, right, or left – and party or coalition affiliations, successful social media campaigns have embraced

---

[19] The confluence of celebrity culture and social media campaigns is evident in the emergence of celebrity politicians, referring to individuals from sports or entertainment backgrounds who transition into politics (see Beta & Neyazi, 2022).

a *populist communication style*. This style involves "adversarial, emotional, patriotic, and abrasive speech through which they connect with the discontented often via grassroots, community-oriented, communicative practices, and spaces" (Block & Negrine, 2017: 182). The populist style is not exclusive to authoritarian figures like Hun Sen but is also adopted by progressive opposition leaders such as Pita Limjaroenrat. In the prevailing *algorithmic marketing culture*, political messages are not treated uniformly. Populist communication stands out due to its heightened potential for visibility, popularity, and virality.

Like the *affective binary framework* for grassroots activism (see Section 4.2.2), social media populist campaigning also emphasizes affective mobilization. *Populist communication style* embraces affect and encompasses emotions and passions as part of its political persuasion, creating a divide between "the elites" and "the people" (Tietjen, 2023). Populist social media campaigns foster a sense of crisis that demands swift collective action by tapping into discontent and frustration, presenting a perception of systemic issues. Anger attributes grievances to "the establishment," while fear broadens the audience by anticipating potential crisis effects. Hence, the *populist communication style* appeals to individual emotions and nurtures a collective identity through empathetic and sympathetic emotions, contributing to the construction of "the people." As such, it aligns well with social media's *algorithmic marketing culture* (see Section 1.3), which tends to favor content with extreme affect, elicit strong reactions, or adhere to the economics of emotion (Lim, 2023a).

In this context, efforts to garner support based on policies, sociopolitical issues, and economic agendas often fall short of evoking strong emotions, diminishing the chances of achieving widespread visibility. On the contrary, affective mobilization that focuses on candidates' personalities, either through positive portrayals or intense personal attacks on their opponents, is more likely to gain viral traction. This is due to its ability to elicit extreme affect, hate or love.

Some leaders, such as Duterte, have taken the *populist communication style* to extreme levels by incorporating vulgar language to establish a connection with ordinary citizens. For instance, in September 2016, Duterte referred to Obama as "a son of a whore" for promising to address the issue of the deadly "drug war." On social media, his supporters highlighted that his use of vulgarity demonstrated authenticity, honesty, and a representation of what ordinary individuals wished to express but hesitated to say. Another facet involves challenging taboos, such as opposing political correctness, by being the first to articulate views considered politically incorrect or impolite, thereby distinguishing oneself from the elite. These elements are strategically employed as they effectively resonate with the limited attention span environment and the prevalent *algorithmic marketing culture* on social media platforms.

5.3 Algorithmic Politics, Social Media Campaign Industry, and Disinformation

From Jokowi's and Prabowo's victories in the Indonesian 2014, 2019, and 2024 elections to Duterte's and Bongbong Marcos' successes in the Philippines' 2016 and 2022 presidential elections, and Hun Sen's achievement in promoting his son, Hun Manet, in the 2023 Cambodian election, the influence of the social media campaign industry and the prevalence of *algorithmic politics* have become evident.

5.3.1 Algorithmic Politics in/for Elections

This increasing integration of *algorithmic politics* in electoral politics is characterized by three key trends. First, there is a notable professionalization and financial backing, signifying the growing sophistication and strategic nature of social media campaigning. Financial support from elite individuals and groups associated with the campaign industry has emerged as a driving force, empowering campaigns to invest substantially in advanced technologies, tools, and expertise (Saraswati, 2020; Wijayanto & Berenschot, 2021).

The political campaign industry, comprising companies and individuals offering services to political parties, utilizes marketing skills, social media, and algorithmic tools to intensify social divisions for power struggles. Services range from political consultancy to image-making, data analytics, and media consultancy, forming interconnected clusters. The industry may consist of polling agencies, big data companies, and digital marketing agencies offering comprehensive digital campaign services to secure a candidate's victory through strategic planning, vision conceptualization, campaigning, and media organization (Saraswati, 2020).

The industry's ability to offer comprehensive services relies not only on political commercialization and shared ideology but also on alliances between candidates and the broader political-economic power held by elites. Consequently, financially robust actors possess greater leverage to capitalize on social media's mobilization effects, mainly through the utilization of *algorithmic politics* that exploits targeted advertising features.

My desk research reveals that financially powerful entities behind Hun Manet and Prabowo Subianto were among the region's top spenders for Meta ads.[20] Just nine months before the Cambodian 2023 election, the Co-Army, Pekpenh Somalina (a Cambodian singer), and an undisclosed account allocated US$889,734 to run 652 advertisements on behalf of Hun Manet. Meanwhile, over a brief span of ninety days (September-December 2023), a total of US$154,458 was expended for

---

[20] Source: Meta Ads Library, www.facebook.com/ads/library/.

1,600 ads for Prabowo Subianto under three accounts, namely: *Bakti Untuk Rakyat, Yayasan Golkar Institut SKP*, and *Indonesia Adil Makmur*. The same accounts collectively allotted more than $1.1 million toward financing over 10,000 ads for Prabowo between August 2020 and December 2023.

The combination of increasing influence through financial means and the rich-get-richer principle of *scale-free* networks contributes to an increasingly unequal social media landscape. This dynamic makes it easier for powerful political actors to exploit and further enhance their influence.

The second trend involves the strategic integration of a paid campaign network aimed at manipulating public discourse. This network typically employs paid *buzzers* or *cyber-troops*, *cyber-trolls*,[21] *bots*,[22] and social media influencers.

In Indonesia, Jokowi's campaign undoubtedly drew strength from genuine grassroots activism, including support from progressive activists and civil society groups. However, it also heavily relied on the marketing strategies of his professional campaigners (Saraswati, 2020) to craft his image, branding him as an "anti-corruption outsider" and a "commoner." In the 2014 and 2019 presidential elections, Jokowi and his rival Prabowo engaged in *algorithmic politics*. Their campaigns not only sought grassroots support but also utilized *cyber-trolls*, *buzzers*, and online influencers (Rakhmani & Saraswati, 2021).

In the Philippines, Duterte's algorithmic political strategy operated through the utilization of paid *cyber-trolls*, flawed reasoning, and propaganda tech-niques, aiming to manipulate public opinions during the 2016 presidential campaign (Ong & Cabañes, 2018; Ong, Tapsell, & Curato, 2019). The cam-paign deployed fake stories on Facebook pages, portraying criminal and social issues, with the ultimate solution being Duterte as president. The campaign gained traction as people shared these stories, unknowingly supporting Duterte's candidacy. Social media became a crucial battleground, with Duterte's supporters becoming active *keyboard warriors*,[23] shaping public discourse by challenging mainstream media and attacking critics. Pro-Duterte social media influencers, such as Mocha Uson and R. J. Nieto, also played significant roles, garnering millions of followers (Tapsell, 2021). The cam-paign's success resulted in these influencers being rewarded with government positions once Duterte took office.

---

[21] *Cyber-troll* is a certain type of *cyber-troops*; it refers to a user, typically anonymous, who posts content or comments purposely to cause a negative reaction or displays hostility toward others.

[22] *Bots* or *social bots* can be defined as "pieces of more or less automated computer software, programmed to mimic the behavior of human internet users" (Larsson & Moe, 2015: 362).

[23] See footnote 7.

The third trend is the predominant use of disinformation, which takes both negative and positive forms. My research in Southeast Asia reveals that social media campaigns often involve clandestine and covert operations that primarily rely on *negative disinformation*. This aligns with Tapsell's (2021) findings that elections have two distinct campaigns: a formal campaign driven by mainstream media and the other involving subversive campaigns on social media platforms based around identity politics and disinformation. However, I also observe that social media campaigns have increasingly become a part of formal and open election campaigns, where *positive disinformation* strategies are utilized quite openly.

The *negative disinformation* tactic is at the heart of most electoral campaigns in the region. The 2014 and 2019 Indonesian presidential election campaigns predominantly revolved around candidates' personalities. They featured personal attacks against the opponent, often accompanied by hate speech, racist and discriminatory messages, and disinformation commonly referred to as a *hoax* in the Indonesian context (Hui, 2020; Leiliyanti & Irawaty, 2020). Such campaigns include accusations against Jokowi, alleging him to be a communist, non-Muslim, and a puppet of a political party, and scrutiny of Prabowo's citizenship, temperament, and his son's sexuality (Hui, 2020).

Following his successful disinformation campaign in 2016, disinformation continued to worsen and manifest in various forms under the Duterte presidency (Chua & Soriano, 2020). Continuing that trend, in the 2022 Philippines presidential elections, Bongbong Marcos' campaign employed damaging disinformation, particularly against his closest rival, Maria Leonor Robredo. Ahead of the elections, some analysts reported that Robredo was the biggest victim of disinformation, with the majority of false information (96 percent) directed against her (Gonzales, 2022). On social media, a slew of doctored photos and videos, some of which went viral, were disseminated to portray Robredo as stupid, unfriendly toward voters, and a communist.

Meanwhile, ahead of the 2022 Malaysian general election, PN coalition leader Muhyiddin exploited Muslim sensitive issues. In a TikTok video that went viral, he made an accusation against rival parties, claiming that they were influenced by Jewish and Christian agents trying to convert Malays from Islam, which is punishable under Islamic laws. The utilization of conspiratorial rhetoric in this campaign is a continuation of and rooted in the entrenched narratives of right-wing Islamist mobilization in the country (Lee, 2010).

As previously mentioned, *positive disinformation* has increasingly been incorporated into social media campaign repertoires. As a manifestation of this tactic, there emerged a campaign method I term *algorithmic whitebranding*, namely, the utilization of digital tools and automated technologies, including AI (artificial intelligence), to create a positive image or brand for a political candidate or public figure who has a deeply controversial or problematic record. The strategy involves more than just whitewashing or historical revisionism, extending to include various political campaigns or public relations strategies aimed at rebranding individuals, distorting the reality (of the present and/or the past), and sanitizing the discourse from any unfavorable aspects. This emerging method has been successfully adopted in recent elections in the Philippines and Indonesia in 2022 and 2024. Both Bongbong and Prabowo effectively utilized *algorithmic whitebranding* to appeal to the public, especially millennial voters who lack memory of their controversial and violent pasts.

The *algorithmic whitebranding* was central in the 2022 Philippines election, where Bongbong Marcos, the son of the late dictator President Ferdinand Marcos, forged an alliance with Duterte's daughter, Sara, as his vice president. In stark contrast to Duterte's polarizing strategy of dividing citizens into "good" individuals and "bad" criminals deserving of death, Bongbong Marcos adopted a reconciliatory stance. Emphasizing unity as the theme across all speeches and interviews, his message aligns with the prevailing "influencer culture of good vibes and toxic positivity" (Curato, 2022). This positive messaging extended to his social media channels, blending political content with cheerful family vlogs (video blogs). On his mother's birthday, BongBong posted a vlog titled "Backstories with Imelda Marcos | Projects During Her Time as First Lady" to remind people of the glorious legacy of his father (Figure 10). With 1.2 million TikTok followers, 2 million YouTube subscribers, and 5.3 million Facebook followers, BongBong Marcos boasted a substantial online presence. Skillfully employing *algorithmic whitebranding*, his campaign resorted to historical distortions, recasting his father's presidency as the Pinoy golden age for peace and infrastructure, sanitizing it from human rights violations and corruption.

The 2024 Indonesian election reveals a parallel scenario as Prabowo Subianto, the son-in-law of the late dictator President Suharto and a former general implicated in genocidal violence, ran with Jokowi's son, Gibran, as his vice president. Unlike Bongbong Marcos, Prabowo did not resort to historical revisionism. Instead, his social media campaign team utilized *algorithmic whitebranding* techniques to rebrand him as a cute and cuddly grandfather figure made for memes, nicknamed *gemoy,* an Indonesian slang word loosely translated as cuddly or huggable. To further soften his image, his white and brown stray cat, Bobby, was included in the campaign with a carefully curated Instagram profile, @bobbykertanegara (Figure 11). There were TikTok videos of Prabowo dancing in a distinctive shuffle style or sending heart-hand gestures toward the audience, rebranding him as a fun-loving old man and distancing him further from his bloody past.

Figure 10 A cover of the "Backstories with Imelda Marcos" vlog

Source: Online capture of www.youtube.com/watch?v=TqWsioSr_GY.

Figure 11 A cartoon depicting Gemoy and Bobby @bobbykertanegara

Source: Online capture of www.instagram.com/bobbykertanegara.

The utilization of *algorithmic whitebranding*, as seen in the cases of Bongbong and Prabowo, was effective not only because it aligned with the *communicative capitalist* logic and the *algorithmic marketing culture* but also because it was strategically employed to appeal to individuals, including the millennials, whose participation in politics is more akin to consumerism rather than citizenship. While both authoritarian leaders won their respective elections, they gained the legitimacy of only some of the population of their countries. Even among the millennials, there were dissents, as evident in numerous calls by Indonesian student executives (BEM, *Badan Eksekutif Mahasiswa*) to reject Prabowo's leadership and a lightning rally of University of the Philippines students against Marcos-Duterte. Arguably, the *algorithmic whitebranding* approach is less likely to influence segments of the population who are critical of autocratic forces and cognizant of their agency as citizens.

5.3.2 Algorithmic Politics for Manipulating the Public Beyond the Elections

Beyond electoral events and amidst vibrant grassroots activism, the increasingly autocratizing regimes and illiberally inclined governments in the region have been employing *algorithmic politics* and leveraging social media mobilization effects to fortify their positions while quashing critics.

In Indonesia, Jokowi's social media campaign networks, including JASMEV, persisted beyond elections, actively campaigning for government policies and suppressing dissent, mainly targeting Islamist critics. During the 2019 #ReformasiDiKorupsi youth movements, the administration utilized social media tactics against student protesters (Section 4.4). This included enlisting influencers to back the controversial bill and deploying *buzzers* to promote the opposing hashtag #SayaBersamaJokowi against #ReformasiDikorupsi.

In that same year, a similar approach was employed to sway public sentiment in favor of the Indonesian government's efforts to limit the authority of KPK, the Corruption Eradication Committee. During this period, numerous Indonesians expressed frustration at what appeared to be a blatant endeavor to weaken the oversight of corrupt politicians. Street protests, led by students, quickly ensued. However, within a few days, the discourse on social media took an unexpected turn, focusing on the peculiar topic of "KPK and Taliban" using hashtag #KPKTaliban and its variations. Utilizing paid *buzzers*, social media platforms were flooded with posts suggesting that the KPK needed restraint due to alleged infiltration by radical Muslims. Despite the seemingly implausible nature of this assertion, the conversation gained traction on Twitter, prompting newspapers to cover the narrative. This online campaign to portray the KPK as "Taliban" played an essential role in swaying public opinion in favor of the government.

In the Philippines, Duterte continued employing *algorithmic politics* through what has been termed the "weaponization of a digital workforce" (Ong & Cabañes, 2018) throughout his presidency. He utilized *keyboard armies* to inundate social media platforms with attacks on critics and posts promoting pro-Duterte sentiment, notably around the "war on drugs." Duterte exploited social media to revive *red-tagging*[24] activists as supporters of the communist insurgency. Human rights activists red-tagged as traitors reportedly faced harassment and even death threats from those accusing them of being unpatriotic. The *red-tagging*, along with the whole suit of *algorithmic politics* practices, continues to be practiced in the presidency of Duterte's successor, Bongbong Marcos.

The military regime in Thailand has systematically developed methods to suppress dissent, where social media plays a crucial role in silencing critics. The Thai state organizes *cyber-troops*, including private traditionalist citizens, to disseminate pro-government messages. These troops monitor and report instances of civic defiance, engage in online bullying and threats against critics, and orchestrate offline harassment campaigns. On platforms like Facebook, *algorithmic enclaves* such as the Social Sanction and the Rubbish Collection Organization effectively mobilize supporters of *lèse majesté*, promoting pro-monarchy and ultraroyalist sentiments (Sombatpoonsiri, 2022).

Employing tactics like *patriotic trolling*, *cyber-troops* in Thailand and the Philippines attack government critics, especially those receiving international funding, presenting it as evidence of their allegiance to the "West" and an act of treason (Sombatpoonsiri, 2018).

In Vietnam, the Communist Party oversees a significant cyber warfare unit, *Force 47* (Lực lượng 47). Introduced in 2017, this military *cyber-army* is dedicated to shaping public opinion on social media platforms and countering what they perceive as "misguided perspectives" online (Reuters, 2017). It does so by deploying spyware on critical government websites to monitor visitors and flooding online spaces with the ruling party's sponsored narratives. Performing *algorithmic whitebranding*, the unit helped the Community Party's attempt to rewrite history by erasing war crimes committed by North Vietnam and the Viet Cong during the Vietnam War. The primary objective is to align historical records with the party's agenda, presenting themselves as the exclusive "heroes" of Vietnam while disregarding alternative viewpoints. Additionally, the unit also employs a tactic like *patriotic trolling* practices in Thailand and the Philippines by

---

[24] *Red-tagging* or *red-baiting* is "the act of labeling, naming, and accusing individuals or groups of being left-leaning communists and enemies of the state" (Lim, 2023b: 41). In the Philippines, *red-tagging* was launched in 1969 as a government-sponsored initiative formulated to counter communist and Maoist factions, specifically targeting the New People's Army. Over time, it has evolved into a detrimental mechanism employed to suppress dissent.

labeling dissenters as "national traitors." These tactics frequently incorporate a hyper/ultranationalist tone, aiming to provoke national outrage and offering a pretext for the government to quash support for democracy and rights.

5.4 The Populist Wave, the Ascendancy of Algorithmic Politics, and Deepening Polarization: A Summary

Insights from Southeast Asia underscore the pivotal role of social media in campaigns, revealing a consistent pattern of heightened division, polarization, and a prevalence of disinformation. This section explores this dynamic, emphasizing that causation cannot be solely attributed to the social media landscape but instead arises from and correlates with three primary factors. First, it stems from the socio-technical consequences of social media and their algorithms. Second, it is grounded in the binary politics of the regions. Third, it is influenced significantly by political actors manipulating the public through *algorithmic politics.*

To highlight, these impacts – polarization and disinformation – socio-technically originate from the *algorithmic marketing culture,* a dialectical interplay between algorithmic operations and marketing principles, mainly branding. In this culture, content's visibility and popularity hinge on its brand performance. Affect, the prevailing currency in social media communication networks, becomes crucial for content virality. This dynamic extends to electoral politics, revealing that political content undergoes scrutiny through the lens of *algorithmic marketing culture,* favoring emotionally charged content – such as those produced within the populist style – over informative political messages.

Furthermore, the escalation of *algorithmic politics* in electoral politics adds fuel to the mix, characterized by the professionalization of campaigns, financial backing, adoption of dual formal and covert strategies, and the incorporation of paid campaign networks, with negative campaigning and *algorithmic white-branding* as dominant strategies. Recently, alongside a significant increase in social media advertising expenditures, the engagement of social media campaign consultants, potentially utilizing advanced technologies such as artificial intelligence, has risen.

Those engaging in *algorithmic politics* harness the algorithmic inclination toward extreme affect within the *algorithmic marketing culture.* They capitalize on the binary nature of politics, enhancing their online visibility not just for electoral gains but also to perpetuate their power and control by segregating citizens into polarized *algorithmic enclaves.* In Southeast Asia, the binary dynamic reflected in electoral politics, combined with the influence of *algorithmic marketing culture,* presents a significant challenge for communities and individuals whose positions differ from those of extreme binary positions. As *algorithmic enclaves* around binary positions gain prominence, social media users with dissenting views become increasingly hesitant to voice their opinions, reflecting a spiral of silence (Noelle-Neumann, 1974), where a reluctance to discuss political issues emerges due to higher perceived disagreement with social ties. The prevalence of *algorithmic politics* is poised to intensify, potentially leading to greater disinformation and deeper polarization.

6 Concluding Remarks

This Element reveals that the intricate interplay between social media and politics in Southeast Asia is multifaceted and co-constituting, sculpted by dynamic technological, sociopolitical, and contextual arrangements. It is situated within and shaped by distinctive national contexts, ever-evolving citizen engagements, and a dynamic political landscape. Nearly four decades since the inception of the internet in the region, a substantial surge in the online population has transpired, hand in hand with an augmented governmental prowess to wield control over technology. Simultaneously, with most of the population active on social media, this digital landscape has experienced heightened commercialization and an increased reliance on algorithms. This has influenced how citizens engage with politics, how political actors interact with citizens, and, ultimately, the trajectory of political developments.

The political implications of social media platforms are multidimensional. While *scale-free* networks contribute to inequality and the consolidation of power, the underlying *platform capitalism* model prioritizes marketing culture over democratic discourse. Notably, social media platforms were not initially conceived with democratic propensity. They predominantly operate as commodified social spheres, where individuals consume, produce, and disseminate information and ideas centered around personal and social pursuits. The intrinsic biases in algorithmic decision-making compound the challenges, intensifying the dominance of *algorithmic marketing culture.*

While social media platforms were initially designed with marketing intentions, that does not mean that marketing logic governs all activities on these platforms. They do not predetermine the outcome of users' actions. Users are not merely passive bystanders without any agency. Instead, collectively, users have the potential to shape the course of events on social media as active citizens rather than passive agents while simultaneously negotiating their positions vis-a-vis algorithmic and marketing predispositions.

In the ever-evolving social media networks, various actors, ranging from individuals and activists to politicians and states, persist in seizing and reshaping digital media to propel their agendas forward. In Southeast Asia, grassroots activism, especially the progressive wing of the youth, have adeptly navigated the intricacies of *communicative capitalist* platforms and, by so doing, have created a space for productive communication and engagement. They employ social media *affordances* that aid groups in confronting collective action problems.

Amidst the evolving social media landscape, characterized by algorithmic biases leaning toward extreme content, challenges emerge for civil society and citizen activism. *Algorithmic marketing culture* can obstruct alignment with democratic and civic objectives. Social media platforms hold the potential to cultivate solidarity, nurturing shared emotions and a collective sense of victimhood. Nevertheless, with the ascent of an *affective binary framework* facilitated by algorithmic dynamics, these platforms can be wielded for hyper/ultranationalist, antidemocratic, and radical right-wing politics. Social media can amplify both progressive and regressive voices, underscoring the significance of discerning the political collectivism it tends to magnify.

Screen interactions possess the dual capacity to bring people together and create divisions. They can shape modes of political involvement and collective activism or potentially intensify polarization as users segregate into exclusionary *algorithmic enclaves*. Within these enclaves, multiple forms of tribal nationalism may emerge, bringing people together through exclusionary solidarity that asserts their privileges while denying the rights of "the Others."

In the tumultuous arena of Southeast Asian politics, social media emerges as a formidable feature for political actors, fueling electoral campaigns with a potent mix of division, polarization, and disinformation. As elections unfold, *algorithmic politics* take center stage, featuring professionalized campaigns, substantial financial backups, and the clandestine maneuvering of paid networks. This orchestrated production is accompanied by a conspicuous surge in social media advertising expenditures, with consultants employing skills and tools to manipulate the narrative, notably through the deployment of negative and positive disinformation strategies.

In Southeast Asia, citizens, activists, and oppositional figures have utilized platforms' *affordances* for building networks, disseminating information, organizing, and mobilizing masses to challenge existing power structures. However, it is essential to acknowledge that technological systems, as embodied in social media platforms, cannot inherently conjure a realm conducive to the flowering of progressive democratization where such conditions do not already exist. More importantly, in isolation, these systems cannot instigate reform in authoritarian regimes resistant to change, especially those adept at employing the same platforms for autocratic and repressive purposes.

Conversely, these technological systems also lack the capacity to automatically shift the political landscape toward authoritarianism if a counterforce, both institutional and grassroots, resists and persists. Lessons learned from recent history show that this resistance may emerge from oppositional forces and/or the progressive digital youth. For Southeast Asia, hope lies not in the hypothetical algorithms of future technological platforms but in the hands of those who adeptly utilize every tool, including technological and digital platforms, to resist looming hegemony. In the dance between technology and politics, the cadence of change may reveal itself. Though the shadows that threaten democracy loom, the unwavering collective fighting for justice may endure.

References

Abbott, J. P. (2011). Cacophony or empowerment? Analyzing the impact of new information communication technologies and new social media in Southeast Asia. *Journal of Current Southeast Asian Affairs, 30*(4), 3–31.

ACLED (2023). *Acled dashboard.* https://acleddata.com/dashboard/#/dashboard.

Adnews (2023). *Nielsen–Digital ad spend in Asia is up 64%.* https://www.adnews.com.au/news/nielsen-digital-ad-spend-in-asia-up-64.

Aichner, T., Grünfelder, M., Maurer, O., and Jegeni, D. (2021). Twenty-five years of social media: A review of social media applications and definitions from 1994 to 2019. *Cyberpsychology, Behavior, and Social Networking, 24* (4), 215–222.

Amnesty International (2021). *Viet Nam: Surge in number of prisoners of conscience, new research shows.* https://www.amnesty.org/en/latest/press-release/2019/05/viet-nam-surge-number-prisoners-conscience-new-research-shows/.

Arugay, A. A., and Baquisal, J. K. A. (2022). Mobilized and polarized: Social media and disinformation narratives in the 2022 Philippine elections. *Pacific Affairs, 95*(3), 549–573.

Asia Centre (2021). *Timor-Leste: Internet freedom under threat.* https://asiacentre.org/wp-content/uploads/Timor-Leste-Internet-Freedoms-Under-Threat.pdf.

Asia Centre (2023). *Internet freedom in Malaysia: Regulating online discourse on race, religion, and royalty.* https://asiacentre.org/wp-content/uploads/Internet-Freedoms-In-Malaysia-Regulating-Online-Discourse-on-Race-Religion-and-Royalty-.pdf.

Aspinall, E., Weiss, M. L., Hicken, A., and Hutchcroft, P. D. (2022). *Mobilizing for elections: Patronage and political machines in Southeast Asia.* Cambridge University Press.

Aung, H. H., and Htut, W. M. (2019). From blogging to digital rights: Telecommunications reform in Myanmar. In L. Brooten, J. M. McElhon, and G. Venkiteswaran (Eds.), *Myanmar media in transition: Legacies, challenges, and change* (pp. 366–376). ISEAS.

Bain & Company (2022). *Southeast Asia's digital consumer: A new stage of evolution.* https://www.edb.gov.sg/content/dam/edb-en/business-insights/market-and-industry-reports/southeast-asias-digital-consumers-a-new-stage-of-evolution/meta_bain_sync_2022.pdf.

Bandial, A. (2019). *Ex-civil servant convicted on sedition charge, sentenced to 18 months.* https://thescoop.co/2019/12/13/ex-civil-servant-convicted-on-sedition-charge-sentenced-to-18-months.

Barabási, A. L., and Albert, R. (1999). Emergence of scaling in random networks. *Science, 286*(5439), 509–512.

Barabási, A. L., and Bonabeau, E. (2003). Scale-free networks. *Scientific American, 288*(5), 60–69.

Barberá, P., and Zeitzoff, T. (2018). The new public address system: Why do world leaders adopt social media? *International Studies Quarterly, 62*(1), 121–130.

Beech, H. (2014). The new face of Indonesian democracy. *Time.* https://time.com/3511035/joko-widodo-indonesian-democracy/.

Benkler, Y. (2006). *The wealth of networks: How social production transforms markets and freedom.* Yale University Press.

Benkler, Y., Faris, R., and Roberts, H. (2018). *Network propaganda: Manipulation, disinformation, and radicalization in American politics.* Oxford University Press.

Bennett, W. L., and Livingstone, S. (Eds.) (2018). *The disinformation age: Politics, technology, and disruptive communication in the United States.* Cambridge University Press.

Beta, A. R., and Neyazi, T. A. (2022). Celebrity politicians, digital campaigns, and performances of political legitimacy in Indonesia's 2019 elections. *International Journal of Communication, 16,* 331–355.

Block, E., and Negrine, R. (2017). The populist communication style: Toward a critical framework. *International Journal of Communication Systems, 11,* 178–197.

Bozarth, L., and Budak, C. (2017). Is slacktivism underrated? measuring the value of slacktivists for online social movements. In *Proceedings of the International AAAI Conference on Web and Social Media, 11*(1), 484–487. https://doi.org/10.1609/icwsm.v11i1.14908.

Bräuchler, B. (2003). Cyberidentities at war: Religion, identity, and the Internet in the Moluccan conflict. *Indonesia, 75,* 123–151.

Bui, T. H. (2016). The influence of social media in Vietnam's elite politics. *Journal of Current Southeast Asian Affairs, 35*(2), 89–111.

Bünte, M. (2020). Democratic backsliding and authoritarian resilience in Southeast Asia: The role of social media. In A. Sinpeng, and R. Tapsell (Eds.), *From grassroots activism to disinformation: Social media in Southeast Asia* (pp. 192–212). ISEAS.

Burgess, J., and Green, J. (2009). *YouTube: Online video and participatory culture.* John Wiley & Sons.

Carr, C. T., and Hayes, R. A. (2015). Social media: Defining, developing, and divining. *Atlantic Journal of Communication, 23*(1), 46–65.

Castells, M. (1996). *The rise of the network society.* John Wiley & sons.

Castells, M. (1997). *The power of identity.* John Wiley & Sons.

Castells, M. (1998). *End of millennium.* John Wiley & sons.

Chak, S. (2014). New information and communication technologies influence on activism in Cambodia. *SUR-International Journal on Human Rights, 11*, 437–447.

Charoenthansakul, T., and Natee, W. (2023). Twitter and the protest movement in Thailand: A thematic analysis of highly retweeted tweets during the pro-democracy protests. *First Monday, 28*(6), 17. https://doi.org/10.5210/fm .v28i6.12666.

Chattharakul, A. (2019). Social media: Hashtag #Futurista. *Contemporary Southeast Asia, 41*(2), 170–175.

Cheong, N. (2020). Disinformation as a response to the "opposition playground" in Malaysia. In A. Sinpeng, and R. Tapsell (Eds.), *From grassroots activism to disinformation: Social media in Southeast Asia* (pp. 63–83). ISEAS.

Chua, L. J. (2012). Pragmatic resistance, law, and social movements in authoritarian states: The case of gay collective action in Singapore. *Law & Society Review, 46*(4), 713–748.

Chua, Y. T., and Soriano, J. C. (2020). Electoral disinformation: Looking through the lens of tsek.ph fact checks. *Plaridel: A Philippine Journal of Communication, Media, and Society, 17*(1), 279–289.

Cossarini, P., and Vallespín, F. (Eds.). (2019). *Populism and passions: Democratic legitimacy after austerity.* Routledge.

Curato, N. (2022). *The Philippines: Erasing history through good vibes and toxic positivity.* https://th.boell.org/en/2022/03/28/philippines-good-vibes-toxic-positivity.

Data Reportal (2023a). *Digital 2023: Global overview report.* https://datarepor tal.com/reports/digital-2023-global-overview-report.

Data Reportal (2023b). *Southeastern Asia.* https://datareportal.com/reports/? tag=Southeastern+Asia.

Dean, J. (2009). *Democracy and other neoliberal fantasies: Communicative capitalism and left politics.* Duke University Press.

Deleuze, G., and Guattari, F. (1987). *A thousand plateaus.* University of Minnesota Press.

Doyle, K. J. (2021). Co-opted social media and the practice of active silence in Cambodia. *Contemporary Southeast Asia, 43*(2), 293–320.

Dubois, E., and Blank, G. (2018). The echo chamber is overstated: The moderating effect of political interest and diverse media. *Information, Communication & Society, 21*(5), 729–745.

Faraj, S., and Azad, B. (2012). The materiality of technology: An affordance perspective. In M. Leonardi, B. A. Nardi, and J. Kallinikos (Eds.), *Materiality and organizing: Social interaction in a technological world* (pp. 237–258). Oxford University Press.

FIDH (2016). *Thailand: Lese-majeste detentions have reached alarming levels, new report says.* www.fidh.org/en/region/asia/thailand/thailand-lese-majeste-detentions-have-reached-alarming-levels-new.

Fraser, N. (1990). Rethinking the public sphere: A contribution to the critique of actually existing democracy. *Social Text, 25/26,* 56–80.

Freedom House (2016). *Thailand.* https://freedomhouse.org/country/thailand/freedom-net/2016.

Freedom House (2022). *Malaysia.* https://freedomhouse.org/country/malaysia/freedom-net/2022.

Freedom House (2023a). *Countries.* https://freedomhouse.org/countries/freedom-net/scores.

Freedom House (2023b). *Brunei.* https://freedomhouse.org/country/brunei/freedom-world/2022.

Freedom House (2023c). *Cambodia.* https://freedomhouse.org/country/cambodia/freedom-net/2023.

Freedom House (2023d). *Indonesia.* https://freedomhouse.org/country/indonesia/freedom-net/2023.

Freedom House (2023e). The *Philippines.* https://freedomhouse.org/country/philippines/freedom-net/2023.

Freedom House (2023f). *Singapore.* https://freedomhouse.org/country/singapore/freedom-net/2023.

Freedom House (2023g). *Vietnam.* https://freedomhouse.org/country/vietnam/freedom-net/2023.

Fuchs, C. (2014). Social media and the public sphere. *TripleC: Communication, Capitalism & Critique, 12*(1), 57–101.

George, C. (2006). *Contentious journalism and the Internet: Towards democratic discourse in Malaysia and Singapore.* NUS Press.

Gerber, A. S., and Green, D. P. (2000). The effects of canvassing, telephone calls, and direct mail on voter turnout: A field experiment. *American Political Science Review, 94*(3), 653–663.

Gonzales, G. (2022). Robredo is top target of disinformation in initiative's January 2022 fact-checks. *Rappler.* www.rappler.com/technology/social-media/leni-robredo-top-target-disinformation-tsek-ph-report.

Govil, N., and Baishya, A. K. (2018). The bully in the pulpit: Autocracy, digital social media, and right-wing populist technoculture. *Communication Culture & Critique, 11*(1), 67–84.

Habermas, J. (1989). *The structural transformation of the public sphere: An inquiry into a category of bourgeois society.* MIT Press.

Hill, D. T. (2002). East Timor and the internet: Global political leverage in/on Indonesia. *Indonesia, 73,* 25–51.

Hindman, M. (2008). *The myth of digital democracy.* Princeton University Press.

Hindman, M. (2018). *The Internet trap: How the digital economy builds monopolies and undermines democracy.* Princeton University Press.

Holt, D. (2016). Branding in the age of social media. *Harvard Business Review, 94*(3), 40–50.

HRW (2024). *Free Vietnam's political prisoners!* https://www.hrw.org/video-photos/interactive/2024/06/05/free-vietnams-political-prisoners.

Huang, K. (2022). *For Gen Z, TikTok is the new search engine.* https://www.straitstimes.com/opinion/for-gen-z-tiktok-is-the-new-search-engine.

Hui, J. Y. (2020). Social media and the 2019 Indonesian elections. *Southeast Asian Affairs*, 155–172.

Hutt, D. (2016). The triangulation of Cambodian politics. *The Diplomat.* https://thediplomat.com/2016/06/the-triangulation-of-cambodian-politics/.

IFJ (2022). *Timor-Leste: Journalist sued over report alleging ministerial corruption.* https://www.ifj.org/media-centre/news/detail/category/press-releases/article/timor-leste-journalist-sued-over-report-alleging-ministerial-corruption.

Johns, A., and Cheong, N. (2019). Feeling the chill: Bersih 2.0, state censorship, and "networked affect" on Malaysian social media 2012–2018. *Social Media+ Society, 5*(2), https://doi.org/10.1177/2056305118821801.

Johns, A., and Cheong, N. (2021). The affective pressures of WhatsApp: From safe spaces to conspiratorial publics. *Continuum, 35*(5), 732–746.

Jordt, I., Than, T., and Lin, S. Y. (2021). *How generation Z galvanized a revolutionary movement against Myanmar's 2021 military coup.* ISEAS.

Jost, J. T., Barberá, P., Bonneau, R., et al. (2018). How social media facilitates political protest: Information, motivation, and social networks. *Political Psychology, 39*, 85–118.

Kemp, S. (2021). The social media habits of young people in Southeast Asia. *Data Reportal.* https://datareportal.com/reports/digital-youth-in-south-east-asia-2021.

Khoo, Y. H. (2020). *The Bersih movement and democratisation in Malaysia: Repression, dissent and opportunities.* Lexington Books.

Koc-Michalska, K., Lilleker, D. G., Surowiec, P., and Baranowski, P. (2014). Poland's 2011 online election campaign: New tools, new professionalism, new ways to win votes. *Journal of Information Technology & Politics, 11*(2), 186–205.

Kusumaryati, V. (2021). # Papuanlivesmatter: Black consciousness and political movements in West Papua. *Critical Asian Studies, 53*(4), 453–475.

Kyaw, N. N. (2020). Social media, hate speech and fake news during Myanmar's political transition. In A. Sinpeng, and R. Tapsell (Eds.), *From *grassroots activism to disinformation: Social media in, Southeast Asia* (pp. 86–104). ISEAS.

Lanham, R. A. (2006). *The economics of attention: Style and substance in the age of information*. University of Chicago Press.

Larsson, A. O., and Moe, H. (2015). Bots or journalists? News sharing on Twitter. *Communications, 40*(3), 361–370.

Lee, J. C. (2010). *Islamization and activism in Malaysia*. ISEAS.

Leiliyanti, E., and Irawaty, D. (2020). Religious and political public sentiment towards political campaign in social media: Indonesia and Malaysia cases. *Humanities & Social Sciences Reviews, 8*(1), 255–263.

Li, C. L. J. (2012). The cyberspace in Brunei. *Asian Politics & Policy, 4*, 127–130.

Lim, J. B. (2017). Engendering civil resistance: Social media and mob tactics in Malaysia. *International Journal of Cultural Studies, 20*(2), 209–227.

Lim, M. (2002). Cyber-civic space in Indonesia: From panopticon to pandemonium? *International Development Planning Review, 24*(4), 383–401.

Lim, M. (2005). *Islamic radicalism and anti-Americanism in Indonesia: The role of the Internet*. East-West Center.

Lim, M. (2013). Many clicks but little sticks: Social media activism in Indonesia. *Journal of Contemporary Asia, 43*(4), 636–657.

Lim, M. (2016). Sweeping the unclean: Social media and the Bersih electoral reform movement in Malaysia. *Global Media Journal, 14*(27), 1–10.

Lim, M. (2017a). Freedom to hate: Social media, algorithmic enclaves, and the rise of tribal nationalism in Indonesia. *Critical Asian Studies, 49*(3), 411–427.

Lim, M. (2017b). Digital media and Malaysia's electoral reform movement. In W. Berenschot, H. Schulte Nordholt, and L. Bakker (Eds.), *Citizenship and democratization in Southeast Asia* (pp. 209–237). Brill.

Lim, M. (2018). Roots, routes, and routers: Communications and media of contemporary social movements. *Journalism & Communication Monographs, 20* (2), 92–136.

Lim, M. (2019). Disciplining dissent: Freedom, control and digital activism in Southeast Asia. In R. Padawangi (Ed.), *Routledge handbook of urbanization in Southeast Asia* (pp. 478–494). Routledge.

Lim, M. (2020a). Algorithmic enclaves: Affective politics and algorithms in the neoliberal social media landscape. In M. Boler, and E. Davis (Eds.), *Affective politics of digital media* (pp. 186–203). Routledge.

Lim, M. (2020b). The politics and perils of dis/connection in the Global South. *Media, Culture & Society, 42*(4), 618–625.

Lim, M. (2023a). "Everything everywhere all at once": Social media, marketing/algorithmic culture, and activism in Southeast Asia. *Georgetown Journal of International Affairs, 24*(2), 181–190.

Lim, M. (2023b). From activist media to algorithmic politics: The Internet, social media, and civil society in Southeast Asia. In M. Weiss, and E. Hansson (Eds.), *Routledge handbook of civil and uncivil society in Southeast Asia* (pp. 25–44). Routledge.

Lindquist, J. (2018). Illicit economies of the internet: Click farming in Indonesia and beyond. *Made in China Journal*, *3*(4), 88–91.

Luong, D. (2020). Social media's challenge to state information controls in Vietnam. In A. Sinpeng, and R. Tapsell (Eds.), *From grassroots activism to disinformation: Social media in Southeast Asia* (pp. 145–166). ISEAS.

Mann, T. (2021). *Attempts to revise draconian ITE law stumble.* https://indone siaatmelbourne.unimelb.edu.au/attempts-to-revise-draconian-ite-law-stumble/.

Manushya Foundation (2023). *Defending digital freedom: ASEAN coalition confronts Laos' social media clampdown.* https://www.manushyafounda tion.org/laossocialmediaclampdown.

Milkman, K. L., and Berger, J. (2012). What makes online content viral. *Journal of Marketing Research*, *49*(2), 192–205.

Momentum Works (2023). *Ecommerce in Southeast Asia.* https://momentum .asia/product/ecommerce-in-southeast-asia-2023/.

Morgenbesser, L. (2016). *Behind the façade: Elections under authoritarianism in Southeast Asia.* State University of New York Press.

Morozov, E. (2011). *The net delusion: The dark side of Internet freedom.* PublicAffairs.

Noelle-Neumann, E. (1974). The spiral of silence a theory of public opinion. *Journal of Communication*, *24*(2), 43–51.

Ong, J. C., and Cabañes, J. V. A. (2018). *Architects of networked disinforma-tion: Behind the scenes of troll accounts and fake news production in the Philippines.* https://doi.org/10.7275/2cq4-5396.

Ong, J. C., and Tapsell, R. (2022). Demystifying disinformation shadow econ-omies: Fake news work models in Indonesia and the Philippines. *Asian Journal of Communication*, *32*(3), 251–267.

Ong, J., Tapsell, R., and Curato, N. (2019). Tracking digital disinformation in the 2019 Philippine Midterm Election. *New Mandala.* https://www.newmandala .org/wp-content/uploads/2019/08/Digital-Disinformation-2019-Midterms.pdf.

Ortmann, S. (2016). Singapore 2011–2015: A tale of two elections. *Asia Maior*, *26*, 197–212.

Palatino, M. (2014). Laos' Internet law undermines free speech. *The Diplomat.* http://thediplomat.com/2014/11/laos-Internet-law-undermines-free-speech.

Pandi, A. (2014). Insurgent space in Malaysia: Hindraf movement, new media and minority Indians. *International Development Planning Review*, *36*(1), 73–90.

Pang, N. (2020). Social media and changes in political engagement in Singapore. In A. Sinpeng, and R. Tapsell (Eds.), *From grassroots activism to disinformation: Social media in Southeast Asia* (pp. 167–191). ISEAS.

Papacharissi, Z. (2009). The virtual sphere 2.0., the Internet, the public sphere, and beyond. In A. Chadwick, and P. N. Howard (Eds.), *Routledge handbook of Internet politics* (pp. 230–245). Routledge.

Pariser, E. (2011). *The filter bubble: How the new personalized web is changing what we read and how we think*. Penguin.

Passeri, A. (2019). New media, old narratives? Myanmar's Internet boom and the spread of anti-Rohingya propaganda on social media. *Geopolitica, 8*(2), 135–156.

Poetranto, I., Lau, J., and Gold, J. (2021). Look south: Challenges and opportunities for the "rules of the road" for cyberspace in ASEAN and the AU. *Journal of Cyber Policy, 6*(3), 318–339.

Power, T. P. (2018). Jokowi's authoritarian turn and Indonesia's democratic decline. *Bulletin of Indonesian Economic Studies, 54(3)*, 307–338.

Rafael, V. L. (2003). The cell phone and the crowd: Messianic politics in the contemporary Philippines. *Philippine Political Science Journal, 24*(47), 3–36.

Rakhmani, I., and Saraswati, M. S. (2021). Authoritarian populism in Indonesia: The role of the political campaign industry in engineering consent and coercion. *Journal of Current Southeast Asian Affairs, 40*(3), 436–460.

Ratcliffe, R. (2022). Fears Cambodia is rolling out China-style "Great Firewall" to curb online freedom. *The Guardian.* https://www.theguardian.com/world/2022/feb/14/fears-cambodia-is-rolling-out-china-style-great-firewall-to-curb-online-freedom.

Reuters (2017). *Vietnam unveils 10,000-strong cyber unit to combat "wrong views."* www.reuters.com/article/us-vietnam-security-cyber/vietnam-unveils-10000-strong-cyber-unit-to-combat-wrong-views-idUSKBN1EK0XN/.

Reuters (2021). *Malaysia seeks stricter Sharia law for "promoting LGBT lifestyle."* www.reuters.com/world/asia-pacific/malaysia-seeks-stricter-sharia-laws-promoting-lgbt-lifestyle-2021-06-24.

Reuters Institute (2022). *Digital news report 2022.* https://reutersinstitute.politics.ox.ac.uk/sites/default/files/2022-06/Digital_News-Report_2022.pdf.

Rio, V. (2021). Myanmar: The role of social media in fomenting violence. In L. Schirch (Ed.), *Social media impacts on conflict and democracy: The tectonic shift* (pp. 143–160). Routledge.

Rodan, G. (2018). *Participation without democracy: Containing conflict in Southeast Asia*. Cornell University Press.

RSF (2003). Vietnam, *reporters without borders.* https://rsf.org/en/country/vietnam.

RSF (2023). 2023 World Press Freedom Index. https://rsf.org/en/2023-world-press-freedom-index-journalism-threatened-fake-content-industry.

Ryan, M., and Tran, M. V. (2022). Democratic backsliding disrupted: The role of digitalized resistance in Myanmar. *Asian Journal of Comparative Politics*, *9*(1), 133–158.

Saraswati, M. (2020). The political campaign industry and the rise of disinformation in Indonesia. In A. Sinpeng, and R. Tapsell (Eds.), *From grassroots activism to disinformation: Social media in Southeast Asia* (pp. 43–62). ISEAS.

Sastramidjaja, Y. (2020). *Indonesia: Digital communications energising new political generation's Campaign for Democracy*. ISEAS-Yusof Ishak Institute. https://www.iseas.edu.sg/articles-commentaries/iseas-perspective/indonesia-digital-communications-energising-new-political-generations-campaign-for-democracy-by-yatun-sastramidjaja/.

Sastramidjaja, Y. (2024). Rhizomatic protest, generational affinity and digital refuge: Southeast Asia's new youth movements. In G. Facal, E.L. de Micheaux, and A. Norén-Nilsson (Eds.), *The Palgrave handbook of political norms in Southeast Asia* (pp. 501–520). Palgrave Macmillan.

Sastramidjaja, Y., and Rasidi, P. R. (2021). The hashtag battle over Indonesia's Omnibus Law: From digital resistance to cyber-control. *ISEAS Perspective* 95. www.iseas.edu.sg/articles-commentaries/iseas-perspective/2021-95-the-hashtag-battle-over-indonesias-omnibus-law-from-digital-resistance-to-cyber-control-by-yatun-sastramidjaja-and-pradipa-p-rasidi/.

Scammell, M. (2007). Political brands and consumer citizens: The rebranding of Tony Blair. *The Annals of the American Academy of Political and Social Science*, *611*(1), 176–192.

Schäfer, S. (2018). Islam in the echo chamber: Ahmadiyya and Shi'a identities in Indonesian and Malaysian online discourses. *Asiascape: Digital Asia*, *5*(1–2), 124–158.

Scheufele, D. A. (2000). Agenda-setting, priming, and framing revisited: Another look at cognitive effects of political communication. *Mass communication & society*, *3*(2–3), 297–316.

Schirch, L. (Ed.). (2021). *Social media impacts on conflict and democracy: The tectonic shift*. Routledge.

Schleffer, G., and Miller, B. (2021). The political effects of social media platforms on different regimes. *Texas National Security Review*, *4*(3), 78–103.

Seto, A. (2017). *Netizenship, activism and online community transformation in Indonesia*. Springer.

Shirky, C. (2011). The political power of social media: Technology, the public sphere, and political change. *Foreign Affairs*, *90*(1), 28–41.

Simpson, B. (2004). Solidarity in the age of globalization: The transnational movement for East Timor and U. S. Foreign Policy. *Peace & Change, 29* (3–4), 349–615.

Singapore Broadcasting Authority (SBA) (2002). *Internet code of practice.* www.sba.gov.sg/sba/i_codenpractice.jsp.

Sinpeng, A. (2020). Digital media, political authoritarianism, and Internet controls in Southeast Asia. *Media, Culture & Society, 42*(1), 25–39.

Sinpeng, A. (2021a). Hashtag activism: Social media and the# FreeYouth protests in Thailand. *Critical Asian Studies, 53*(2), 192–205.

Sinpeng, A. (2021b). *Opposing democracy in the digital age: The yellow shirts in Thailand.* University of Michigan Press.

Sinpeng, A., and Tapsell, R. (Eds.). (2020). *From grassroots activism to disinformation: Social media in Southeast Asia.* ISEAS.

Smeltzer, S. (2008). Blogging in Malaysia: Hope for a new democratic technology? *Journal of International Communication, 14*(1), 28–45.

Sombatpoonsiri, J. (2018). *Manipulating civic space: Cyber trolling in Thailand and the Philippines.* www.ssoar.info/ssoar/handle/document/57960.

Sombatpoonsiri, J. (2022). We are independent trolls: The efficacy of royalist digital activism in Thailand. *ISEAS Perspective 1.* www.iseas.edu.sg/articles-commentaries/iseas-perspective/2022-1-we-are-independent-trolls-the-effi cacy-of-royalist-digital-activism-in-thailand-by-janjira-sombatpoonsiri/.

Spohr, D. (2017). Fake news and ideological polarization: Filter bubbles and selective exposure on social media. *Business Information Review, 34*(3), 150–160.

Srnicek, N. (2017), *Platform capitalism.* John Wiley & Sons.

Striphas, T. (2015). Algorithmic culture. *European Journal of Cultural Studies, 18*(4–5), 395–412.

Suiter, J. (2016). Post-truth politics. *Political Insight, 7*(3), 25–27.

Sunstein, C. R. (2018). Is social media good or bad for democracy? *International Journal of Human Righ*ts, *15*(27), 83–89.

Suwana, F. (2020). What motivates digital activism? The case of the Save KPK movement in Indonesia. *Information, Communication & Society, 23* (9), 1295–1310.

Tapsell, R. (2017). *Media power in Indonesia: Oligarchs, citizens and the digital revolution.* Rowman & Littlefield.

Tapsell, R. (2021). Social media and elections in Southeast Asia: The emergence of subversive, underground campaigning. *Asian Studies Review, 45*(1), 117–134.

Teeratanabodee, W., and Wasserstrom, J. (2024). How repression (and protest) gets repeated. *Journal of Democracy.* www.journalofdemocracy.org/online-exclusive/how-repression-and-protest-gets-repeated/.

Thayer, C. A. (1992). *Political developments in Vietnam: From the sixth to seventh National Party Congress*. https://openresearch-repository.anu.edu.au/bitstream/1885/133711/1/Political_Developments_in_Vietnam.pdf.

The Scoop (2023). *About us*. https://thescoop.co/about/.

Tietjen, R. R. (2023). The affects of populism. *Journal of the American Philosophical Association*, *9*(2), 284–302.

TLHR (2021). *The number of prosecutions under lèse-majesté in 2020–2021*. https://tlhr2014.com/en/archives/24103.

Twiplomacy (2020). *Twiplomacy study 2020*. https://www.twiplomacy.com/twiplomacy-study-2020.

Tye, M., Leong, C., Tan, F., Tan, B., and Khoo, Y. H. (2018). Social media for empowerment in social movements: The case of Malaysia's grassroots activism. *Communications of the Association for Information Systems*, *42*(15), 408–430.

Ufen, A. (2017). Political finance and corruption in Southeast Asia: Causes and challenges. In M. dela Rama, and C. Rowley (Eds.), *The changing face of corruption in the Asia Pacific* (pp. 23–33). Elsevier.

V-Dem (2023). *Democracy report 2023: Defiance in the face of autocratization*. www.v-dem.net/documents/29/V-dem_democracyreport2023_lowres.pdf.

Vong, M., and Sinpeng, A. (2020). Cambodia: From democratization of information to disinformation. In A. Sinpeng, and R. Tapsell (Eds.), *From grassroots activism to disinformation: Social media in Southeast Asia* (pp. 126–144). ISEAS.

Vu, N. A. (2017). Grassroots environmental activism in an authoritarian context: The trees movement in Vietnam. *VOLUNTAS: International Journal of Voluntary and Nonprofit Organizations*, *28*, 1180–1208.

Wallace, J. (2017). *With social media, Vietnam's dissidents grow bolder despite crackdown. New York Times*. www.nytimes.com/2017/07/02/world/asia/vietnam-mother-mushroom-social-media-dissidents.html.

Weiss, M. L. (2014). New media, new activism: Trends and trajectories in Malaysia, Singapore and Indonesia. *International Development Planning Review*, *36*(1), 91–109.

Weiss, M. L. (2023). Scapegoating queers: Pink-blocking as state strategy. *Current Sociology*, https://doi.org/10.1177/00113921231217498.

Weiss, M. L., and Suffian, I. (2023). Decline, fall, and resurrection of a dominant-coalition system: Malaysia's tortured partisan path. *Pacific Affairs*, *96*(2), 281–301.

Wijayanto and Berenschot, W. (2021). The organisation and funding of social media propaganda. *Inside Indonesia*, *146*. https://www.insideindonesia.org/

editions/edition-146-oct-dec-2021/organisation-and-funding-of-social-media-propaganda.

World Bank (2023). *GDP per capita (current US$)*. https://data.worldbank.org/indicator/NY.GDP.PCAP.CD.

World Bank (2024). *Data*. https://data.worldbank.org/indicator.

World Population Review (2023). *Asia population*. https://worldpopulationreview.com/continents/asia-population.

Zeitzoff, T. (2017). How social media is changing conflict. *Journal of Conflict Resolution*, *61*(9), 1970–1991.

Zhang, W. (2016). Social media and elections in Singapore: Comparing 2011 and 2015. *Chinese Journal of Communication*, *9*(4), 367–384.

Zuiderveen Borgesius, F., Trilling, D., Möller, J., et al. (2016). Should we worry about filter bubbles? *Internet Policy Review: Journal on Internet Regulation*, *5*(1), 1–16.

Acknowledgments

First and foremost, I thank the series editors, Meredith L. Weiss and Edward Aspinall, for their unwavering trust and generosity. In an ideal world, this Element would have been published years earlier, but unexpected turns in life dramatically changed my timeline. Opportunities for second chances have been scarce, and a third chance was never granted. Therefore, the extraordinary opportunity the editors granted me – a fourth chance – is something I truly hold dear. Special appreciation is extended to Meredith, who was my primary point of contact. I am immensely grateful for her exceptional support and kindness.

I extend sincere thanks to the three anonymous reviewers for their encouraging feedback and invaluable constructive suggestions.

I owe thanks to the Carleton Fall 2023 Graduate Writing Bootcamp fellows for their companionship and encouragement, which were pivotal in jumpstarting my return to intensive writing.

Special gratitude goes to James O'Halloran, Dr. Trangmar, Dr. Chang, Dr. Le, Dr. Fung, Dr. Lynn, Dr. Lamensa, Dr. Lorimer, Dr. Davies, Dr. Meulenkamp, K. McRae, and the excellent staff at the Ottawa Hospitals, notably the Cancer Centre at the General Campus and the University of Ottawa Heart Institute. Their essential support and assistance were indispensable; without them, quite literally, this Element would never have come to fruition.

The research for this Element, in part, is funded by the Canada Research Chairs and SSHRC Insight Grant #435–2017-1470.

Dedicated to all Southeast Asians who persist in the fight for justice.

For EU product safety concerns, contact us at Calle de José Abascal, 56–1°,
28003 Madrid, Spain or eugpsr@cambridge.org.